BOB ROLL

BOBKE II

★ ★ ★

VELO press.

Bobke II *is a compilation of articles and journals published in* VeloNews *since 1996. Part I was previously published as* Bobke *(VeloPress®, 1995).*

Distributed in the United States and Canada by Publishers Group West.

International Standard Book Number: 1-931382-28-X

Library of Congress Cataloging-in-Publication Data available

VeloPress®
1830 North 55th Street
Boulder, Colorado 80301–2700 USA
303/440-0601 • Fax 303/444-6788 • E-mail velopress@7dogs.com

To purchase additional copies of this book or other VeloPress® books, call 800/234-8356 or visit us on the Web at velopress.com.

Cover: Front cover foreground photo by Malcolm Fearon/Bliss Images. Background photos on front and back covers by Tom Moran/Singletrack Photography.

Cover and interior design and composition by Erin Johnson.

Praise for *Bobke: A Ride on the Wild Side of Cycling*

"Bob has a fine eye for the absurd nature of racing a bicycle for a living."

—**Ned Overend**, professional mountain bike racer

"All things considered, Bob is a pretty damn good writer."

—**Daryl Price**, professional mountain bike racer

"Bob Roll is the consummate team player and one of the most 'gentle-manly' riders that I know of in the peloton. He has suffered through countless races helping riders such as Andy Hampsten win the Giro with nary a whimper about how little exposure he gained for his toils.
He followed the 'code of respect' that the European 'profis' demanded of their peers. Bob was always there when you needed him but never in the way! The consummate professional."

—**Alex Stieda**, former 7-Eleven teammate of Bob Roll

"Not a day passes in the life of Bob Roll without a little good time commotion."

—**Todd Balf**, *Outside* magazine

☆ ☆ ☆   CONTENTS   ☆ ☆ ☆

Foreword *by Dan Koeppel* . . . . **vii**

PART I

1. Way Out West **3**
2. The Day the Big Men Cried **15**
3. One Racer's View **21**
4. Believe or Leave **24**
5. Blind Faith Was My Motto at the '86 Tour **36**
6. Springtime in Hell **41**
7. Bobke on the Defensive **62**
8. Lost in the Jemez **70**
9. Bobke Takes to the Dirt **77**
10. Deep Down Dirty with Bobke **83**
11. Living in a Lactic-acid Crippling Haze **92**
12. Euro' Trashed **98**
13. Dream Season **106**
14. Nerves + Neurosis **113**
15. Rhythm is a Racer **120**
16. The Watch **125**

CONTENTS

☆ ☆ ☆   ☆ ☆ ☆

PART II

17. The Sport According to Bobke **133**

18. The "Water Hole" Revisited **136**

19. One Heli Tour **139**

20. Bobke's Back! **144**

21. Dry Bread Wants a Harley **146**

22. Lance and the Dipped in Ding-dong Doodle
    Down in Dixie **149**

23. Nine Guesses **161**

24. A Day at the Fair **163**

25. The Night before Amstel. **170**

26. Into the Twenty-first Century **173**

27. 51 Things to Do before You Die **178**

28. Eurotrash and the Texas Tornado **184**

29. Training Tips with Bobke **187**

30. Il Becco Bartalese, Following in Coppi's and
    Bartali's Tracks **191**

About the Author. **195**

OWN THE ROAD, DANNY BOY! OWN THE ROAD!" This was the moment—driving my non-high performance Honda Civic wagon down Interstate 5, heading toward the annual bike industry trade show in Anaheim, California—that I knew the maniac screaming directions in my back seat was somebody I wanted to be friends with. Bob Roll had been staying with a mutual buddy, and he'd hitched a ride with me; all I knew about him was that he'd raced the Tour de France, then gone on to become a pro mountain biker. I'd seen him the summer earlier at a World Cup race in Mammoth, California. He was contending for a top-10 placement, just a few hundred yards from the finish line, when he flatted. I watched him as he struggled to change his tire. There was a furious look on his face—that mask of pain, determination, and anger that all bike racers wear.

Get to know this guy? He scared the daylights out of me!

Ten years later, I'm still happily afraid.

Bob scares me with his wit. Talk to Bob, and you'll feel you've been given the key to a bank vault filled with a currency you've never heard of—but which you know is priceless.

Take Bob's instant assessment of the difference between European and American pros, an impromptu five-liner as we ogled passers-by in a New York City coffee shop: "In America, bike racing has the veneer of speed and elegance; mostly educated, bourgeois types are attracted to it. In Europe, cycling is grittier and more real. The preconception in the States is that the sport is very Continental, very romantic, but the fact is that the sport's main nature is working class. The Tour de France, especially, exemplifies this. The public loves the event because they know what the riders are going through for them, and that the sport—a concentrated version of the struggles they endure every day—adds value and hope to those struggles."

One of the greatest—and most exclusive, until recently—experiences a bike fan could have was to watch the Tour de France with the sound turned down, as Bob offered his hilarious, insightful, substitute analysis (with his current gig at the Outdoor Life Network, now millions can share this sublime experience).

Bob scares me with his ability be himself, which often means bucking authority, taking the harder path. He never won a stage in the Tour de France, never won a NORBA national mountain bike race, but he established one of the longest pro careers in the history of the sport—because he didn't know when to quit, and didn't want to. (For the record, Bob's official stats are staggering, despite the lack of podium time: He began road racing in 1981 and went to Europe in 1985, competing for team 7-Eleven, Motorola, and Z—in four Tours de France. He raced the Paris-Roubaix seven times, and a Graham Watson photograph of him, nearly skidding off the cobbles, is one of the most exciting cycling action shots I've ever seen. Bob was the first American bike racer to compete in both the French classic and an off-road World Cup race. His only podium appearance? At the 1995 Spokane NORBA national as the fifth American.)

In other words, Bob is that archetypal cyclist/laborer he describes: somebody who works—hard—with what he's been given and stays in the game longer than the elite, "gifted naturals" who seem to think their success is predestined.

Bob scares me with his talent. In 1997, I was hired to edit a new action sports magazine; the first thing I did was to ask Bob to write a few guest columns. One of the editors—a non-cyclist—approached me when Bob turned in his copy; it was fragmented, scrawled on napkins and scraps of paper. "This is unacceptable," he said, dumping the "mess" on my desk.

Mess? It was pure gold. Bob was exhorting all riders to find their inner . . . something. I didn't totally understand it, but it was brilliant:

"You, too, can regain the floating equilibrium of your womb origins. Go out to the trails. Get down on your hands and knees and feel the soil, smell it, run your fingers and toes through it. Divine intervention will come and, like me, you will transcend the constraints modern living imposes on every post-aquatic human embryo. But let me admonish you also to give back what you take from nature, or we shall all perish in a car-mageddon fire, one that's already threatening us from every direction. From his footprint we know Hercules. But for the divine flyers we want and really need to become, the whole is revealed by each, separately and together."

Real writing is prose that reveals something about the person who created it, and that tells us something more about ourselves.

And cracks us the hell up.

Bob is the real deal. I consider myself lucky to know Bob Roll, and I remain an awestruck fan. And it has almost nothing to do with bikes. It has to do with the life he's led, in which bikes happen to be included: He's been a loyal friend and an amazing teacher. Most of all, he's a reminder—to all of us—that we should do what we love, and rigorously steer clear of drudgery, ennui, the grind; if we're not lucky enough to die wealthy, we will at least die very, very happy.

Own the road? Impossible. I only lease it from Bobke. Keep reading, and you'll get in on that rental, too.

— Dan Koeppel

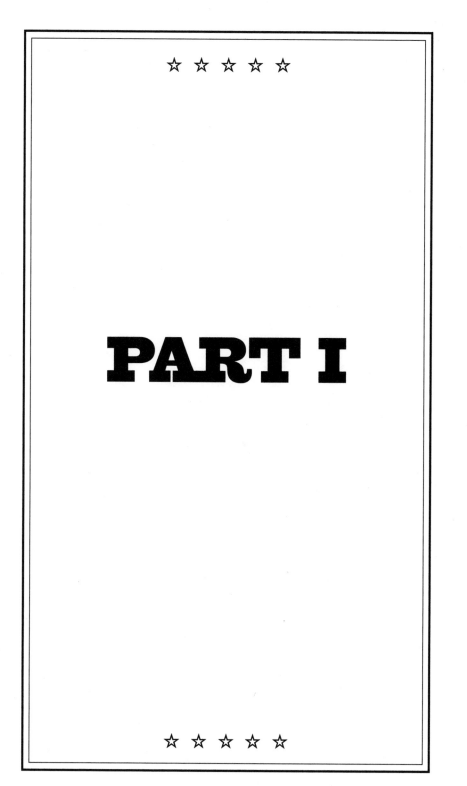

PART I

CHAPTER 1

Way Out West

May 15, 1982

Driving north on I-5 in a hippie-mobile loaded to the gills with the bikes and bikers. Me, Phil "Woo Woo" Wosley, and "Allez" Mark Cahn are traveling north to the biker metropolis of Etna, California, to stay at Mike Neel's house and prepare for the Coors Classic. In Yreka, we stopped at the Roach Diner for the greasiest gut-bomb burgers I ever ate. They make the swill I serve at Perkos Koffee Kup taste like filet mignon at the Cordon Blue. Got to Etna at 2 a.m. and remembered I forgot to get Mike's address. Sheeit. So I go to this bar and ask. Open the door and forty lumberjacks all stop what they are doing and look at me. I look back. I guess I look white trashy enough and don't get chainsawed in the Trinity Alps, shit. The bartender says Mike lives over there. Thanks, etc. . . . As I hit the hay, them hamburgers are doing triple-back sommies in my belly. Geez, I feel dizzy.

May 16

Woke up to a glorious day and we all went out bikin'. The idea is to have us up here at some decent altitude for a couple of weeks to get ready for the Coors Classic in Boulder, starting June 18. Geez, I've got to get in shape. We rode down to this "town" called Fort Jones—and looked at all the locals—"hi there." We kinda stick out like a thumb that has just been crushed by a 20-pound sledge.

May 17

Did an incredibly beautiful ride in the mountains around here. We rode west to a micro town called Callahan, then north over this hill, then down to the Salmon River, which was gorgeous. We stopped for lunch in Forks of Salmon and prayed we wouldn't get shot by any of the local growers. Then we rode back to Etna on this totally cool dirt road over Etna Mountain. I stopped to wait on top and, hoping for some water, flagged down these Baba Ram Bonehead, freaked-out, logger-grower hippies, who stopped their calendars in 1968. All they had was Annie Green Springs wine and some local reefer. I said, thanks anyway.

May 18

Mellow ride due to fatigue. Just cruisin' the Scott River Valley. The locals are getting used to us and have holstered their guns. After dinner, we went down to the local watering hole. So me and Mark Cahn were playin' some pool and Woo Woo was skatin' on some very thin ice talking to this local woman. These two burly loggers came in and challenged me and Allez to some pool. We said fine. They were creaming us and had knocked all their solids down before we got a single stripe to go in. The biggest, ugliest guy then nailed the eight in the corner. The cue ball hit the far bumper and slithered through all seven of our balls and plopped down into the far corner. The logger at the bar didn't even look up to see if they had scratched, 'cause he could hear his partner's cue stick splintering to bits. Me and Mark exchanged sly smiles and made five bucks apiece and split. When the woman Woo Woo was talkin' to found out he didn't chew tobacco or poach deer or drive a pick-up, Woo Woo struck out like Casey at the Bat.

May 19

130-mile, all-day-long ride—up into Oregon by Ashland and all over the place. I felt okay, but Woosley was flying and tried to tear me and Mark's legs off. We had a great time dodging the scourge of Nor Cal: gigantic Winnebagos driven by blue-haired maniac escapees from retirement communities all over America. Anyway, we survived the ride and cruised to Etna—which is a nice place to live, but pretty hard to visit, man.

☆   ☆   ☆

We had a great time dodging gigantic Winnebagos driven by blue-haired maniac escapees from retirement communities all over America.

May 20

Some of the other guys got to town for the Tour of Ashland. Toby Power and Ned Gallagher showed up, and Norm Alvis. The house is getting crowded. You got a bunch of guys shaving their legs and riding bicycles and listening to strange music. So the neighbors are getting a little uneasy and hope we clear out soon.

May 21

Stage 1, Tour of Ashland

We did this lame criterium around the park in the town of Ashland, Oregon. There were around nine spectators—not counting relatives. I got a flat and hid in the bushes so I wouldn't be docked a lap for mechanicals. Hope I don't get poison oak or something.

May 22

Pretty hard road race, and David Mayer-Oakes took off with Woo Woo and they killed everyone. Our team did pretty good today and Mike is happy, I guess. He and his wife and daughter came up from his warehouse in Reno to see who should race the Coors.

May 23

We raced to the top of Mount Ashland, and I wanted to do good. So at the bottom I attacked and nobody caught up to me, so I won by myself about two minutes ahead. I couldn't believe it. So rode back to the hotel in Ashland and cruised into my room feeling pretty happy. There was chain grease on the walls, bikes in the bathroom, blood on the towels from road rash, and garbage from the ten guys staying in two rooms. The manager was a gigantic, bearded version of Norman Bates; he was pacing back and forth between our rooms, lividly cursing all bikers. I didn't say a word, but started cleaning up as fast as I could. The rest of the guys were happy to be having a nice snack by the pool counting their primes. I was happy to be with the living.

May 24

This was a cool road race because our team was in a six-man breakaway. I mean, six of us were in a six-man break from the first hill to the finish. I hope we can do half this good at the Coors.

May 25

Back to Etna, California, at Mike Neel's house. Every cyclist in Nor Cal is staying here, and it is tense. Mike's wife is not too happy to have her house overrun by gigantic termites, who live off pasta and meat and fart a lot and play loud rock. I guess most guys do not think of themselves as larvae, but hey, we're all lucky that pterodactyls are no longer ruling the skies.

June 6

Driving to Colorado with teammates to Copper Mountain for the Coors Classic. Us city boys are stayin' at a condo, owned by the family that is sponsoring our team. I can't believe I am going to do the Coors. But when we went for a ride, I was swimming down the road in a haze of oxygen debt. I've never been to Colorado or this altitude, and I am nervously dying of pulmonary edema. I walked up the stairs to our condo and passed out cold. If I don't adjust soon, I will be dead bloody meat, boys and girls.

June 7

Just about to explode from anxiety. Tomorrow is the prologue. So I rode over the hill we are going to race up. We start at this cool restaurant and climb up this hill called Flagstaff. I just pedaled around Boulder and had a great time eating pretzels and drinking lemonade with a bunch of tie-dyed Deadheads playing Frisbee in front of the courthouse. In the afternoon, we all went to this reception at the Coors Brewery in Golden. Gawd, what a smelly place. A bunch of people were giving speeches, which were probably real interesting, but their words were quivering with a strange drawl and so laden with barometric pressure, I could not understand anything. I guess I'm ready to race.

June 8

Prologue, the Coors Classic

All right! Finally got this race started. I went as fast as I possibly could . . . and I still got slaughtered by Steve Bauer, who is on the Mengoni team. They also have Jacques Boyer and Harvey Nitz, Wayne Stetina, Mayer-Oakes, and this madman named Alexi Grewal. I have heard of him, but today I heard him. He was screaming at the top of his lungs at some poor mechanic for some reason. I am going to try not to make him mad at me.

June 9

Boulder Mountain Road Race

Well, today I went harder than I've ever gone in my life, up this climb to Wondervu. God, I was gagging. Two Colombians, Martin Ramirez and

Patro Jimenez, and Mexican Norbert Caceres flew up the hill and nobody could catch them: They killed everyone and won by three minutes. I was in the main group, with some of the best cyclists around, until I flatted.

June 10

Drove to Estes Park, up in the mountains, for a circuit race. Boyer won the stage, and I was just barely hanging on! I was crossed-eyed trying to stay on the wheel in front of me. Gawd, I hope I feel better soon. If I don't, I'll be a short-order cook at Perkos for the rest of my life.

June 11

Oh my God. I think I'm going to die. Did a race over these mountains from Golden to Vail Pass. My legs are so sore I can't believe it. I don't know if I'll be able to finish this stage race. I do not want to quit, but I don't want to die, either. The Colombians are killing everyone.

June 12

Vail Crit

I never thought 50 miles could be nearly fatal. Vail is at eight or so thousand feet, and I swear I just couldn't breathe. While my teammates are wondering who is doing well on G.C., I am wondering what town I'm in, what day it is, why I can't walk, and what the hell I'm doing in a Colorado bike race.

June 13

A double stage and I'm seeing twice as many stars as usual. We did a hard circuit race called the Tour of the Moon, which Ron Hayman won. I felt better today and didn't get dropped—for the first time in this race. I barely avoided a huge pile-up, but bumped into a guy named Tom Prehn.

Neither of us fell, but he seemed to feel the crash was my fault and said, "You don't belong in this race." I said, "One more word from you and I'll break your kneecap." In the evening, we did a fast crit, won by Alex Stieda. There were twelve turns in 0.9 miles, and I am dizzy as M. Monroe in "Some Like it Hot."

June 14

McClure Pass Road Race

I was pedaling along today and all of a sudden, a herd of horses jumped over the fence and started running along in the pack. That wasn't too bad, but they started shitting all over the place and then, they all got the bonk and started slowing down. Then when we would try to get around them, they started sprinting desperately. I started to get nervous and went to the back of the pack. There was a huge crash; I went down hard and started bleeding all over the place. The pack split up and I was happy to miss the split. Then we finished up this big hill and I went to the doctor to get stitched up. Since they had no pain killers, it was quite painful. I guess I'll survive. The Colombians are really killing everyone now.

June 15

Doing a circuit race today called Suicide Hill. That is no joke—the course was straight up, then straight down, and the Colombians romped again. I didn't feel too bad, but on the second lap, I missed the turn at the bottom of the hill and went flying into the crowd. I landed in the bleachers on top of some spectators, who were totally freaked out. I didn't get hurt, so I got back up and kept going. This afternoon, we did an uphill time trial, and I felt pretty good. I caught my one-minute man and finished 17th. Feeling better now in the races . . . or maybe everyone has come down to my exhausted level.

June 16

We had a criterium today in Denver. There were a ton of crashes and I moved up to 27th place on G.C. This Canadian Hayman won again—in a crazy sprint that I watched from about 50 guys back.

June 17

Morgul-Bismarck Road Race

A huge storm blew in last night and this was one miserable, nasty race. But the elevation is less here, and I can breathe a lot better. So I hung in the main group, got 11th on the stage and moved up to 20th on G.C. The pack blew to bits, and a Russian guy named Viktor Demidenko won the stage— but the Colombians are still killing on G.C.

June 18

Last Day

I was hoping to do this criterium nice and mellow, but instead, I couldn't stay upright. I crashed three times, tore open my stitches, and bled all over the place. Still, I got up each time and caught the group, so I wouldn't lose any laps. I tried to go for a prime $50—but I got creamed by Davis Phinney, who put a finger up and put it down like a cash register. I hope Davis needs them $50 as bad as I do. Anyway, the Coors is over. I'm going back to California to try to heal my wounds.

March 1–3, 1993

Took a Greyhound bus to Reno, Nevada, from Oakland, to meet Norm Alvis. Piles of busted, flat, hung-over gamblers were breathing whisky on me while I waited. Yummy. Norm picked me up and we went to the warehouse in Sparks. We were supposed to pick up a car and drive to Austin,

Way Out West

Texas, for the Tour of Texas. Our coach called the promoter and told him we were coming. Then he gave us this grocery bag full of weed as our housing and entry fee. We stuffed it at the bottom of the trunk and split. We drove out of Reno past the Mustang Ranch and had no thoughts of stopping. Then we turned right on Highway 95, and headed south. We drove across the desert for hours into the night.

We got to Las Vegas at about 3 a.m., got our bikes out and started racing around the streets. There were so many lights we could see fine. We kept driving and stopped at Hoover Dam and took a piss that fell about three miles. We took turns driving and sleeping across Arizona and New Mexico, then pulled off the highway in Fort Stockton, Texas, to gas up. As we left, I forgot to put on the lights, so a cop pulled us over about a half-block later. Norm was very nervous, due to our cargo. I said relax, and don't say anything. The cop wanted to know what two skinny California white boys were doing in the middle of nowhere, driving at night without our lights. After I explained where we were going, he said, "Good luck in the race . . . and keep the lights on at night." I was sweating and relieved to be back on the highway. We kept driving.

We'd been in the Peugeot 205, which shimmied down the road at a maximum of 45 mph, for about 38 hours—and I was getting groggy. About 10 miles past the Davy Crockett Monument, I fell fast asleep at the wheel. I woke up heading for some trees, jerked the steering wheel back toward the highway, and flew across a few lanes of traffic—scaring the crap out of some truckers and myself. Norm never even woke up.

We finally rolled into Austin, totally wasted. We were early for registration, so we waited under the street in a drainage ditch, because it was about 95 degrees. Then we went to the office of the Tour of Texas, got the bag out of the trunk, and walked in. The secretary had her eyes on the desk, and jumped about five feet when she got a look at us. We were filthy—with long, straggly hair, jeans, boots, chipped teeth—and we had these tufts of hair on our chins like Greg Allman. I leaned toward her and said, "We'd like to register." She told us to walk right into the promoter's office. We told the promoter who we were and gave him the bag. He entered us, and got us housing. We got to our condo and went to sleep.

March 4

Prologue, Tour of Texas

Tried to go hard, but wound up with a slow time anyway. My legs were heavy and felt as if somebody poured half-a-ton of lead into each. My lungs got torched nicely, so I had a pleasant afternoon of coughing up phlegm. Took a nap that led straight into 14 hours of sleep. I guess staying awake driving for three days takes some getting used to. . . .

March 5

Bizarre road race up and back along the freeway. We pedaled up the slow lane, did a U-turn, then pedaled down the fast lane all afternoon. I tried to finish even though it was freaking hot. I finished all right, but was so dehydrated I cramped up until I looked like a crayfish or, as they say down here, a crawdaddy.

March 17

Dublin to Fort Worth Road Race

This was normally supposed to be about an 80-mile road race, but only about ten guys finished. The rest of us were out of the race and into the following bus after about two miles. There was a 40-mph crosswind and the 7-Eleven guys went wild from the start. All the bikers in the bus were hacking phlegm and choking on their own spit. Jeff Bradley, from 7-Eleven, won the stage. What a surprise.

March 19

Convention Center Crit

We raced around this parking lot and then went into a parking garage that was unlit—until this Polish guy crashed and sent a shower of sparks into the pack. We rode around these cones, and some 7-Eleven guy won. Me and Norm have been driving all over the western states and have not made one single penny. At least the race lasted long enough for me to get my feet in the toe straps.

March 20

Dallas Crit

I felt good today and got sixth place. I was in shock. I collected my $80 prize money and went to this turn-of-the-century-style steak house, and me and Norm had some meat. As an added bonus, our waitress got on this swing that was attached to the ceiling and started swinging around the restaurant. Me and Norm laughed and ate steak and dodged flying waitresses and had a good ol' time.

March 22

Rode over to Camp Mabry for a lame crit. We've been doing these strange races for a few weeks. This evening, though, a huge thunderstorm blew in. They let us start, but the entire field crashed in the first corner, because it was as slick as snot. I have never seen so many bikes in a pile, ever. They canceled this race and Norm was frowning because he was the only guy who didn't fall.

April 2

Last day of the Tour of Texas

We had a race in downtown Austin on Pecan Street. I didn't feel too bad and was racing near the front when I hit this barrier with my foot. Ouch! Me and Norm packed up and split. Drove straight through to Los Angeles, then north along I-5 for Easter at home.

April 16

Just won the Devil's Cup Hill Climb up Mount Diablo. I felt great and made $1,000. Mike Neel and I had been figuring out how to win this race. I'd ridden up every hill in the Bay Area since I got back from Texas. This hill is practically in my backyard, and a newspaper I used to deliver is the sponsor. So I was really nervous this morning. We started pretty fast, and George Mount was making the tempo. Pretty soon, only about six guys were left at the front. With about 200 yards to go, up this real steep part, I started sprinting. I never went that fast up a hill before, and I creamed 'em. My family got to see me on TV. This sport ain't so bad after all. . . .

★ ★ ★ ★ ★ ★

CHAPTER 2

The Day the Big Men Cried

June 5, 1988

Chiesa Valmalenco to Bormio, Giro d'Italia, Stage 14

In Europe, we are called the "Giants of the Road." At least, that's how the cycling stars are revered in the press and in the hearts of the *tifosi*. As the 7-Eleven team, however, we were perceived as gifted interlopers, racing in Europe for kicks and cash. Our successes were more like stab wounds—a win here and there—than mortal blood-spilling slices to the jugular. But the Gavia Pass stage of the 1988 Giro changed all that. During one of the most dramatic days in the history of cycling, we cracked the chest of European road racing and feasted on its heart.

Before the Gavia stage, increasingly heavy clouds, mean and dark as black leather, had been gathering for days. And the night before, as we reviewed the stage to Bormio, the clouds opened up and a cold rain hammered down. Clearly, the stage was going to be an epic . . . and Drew let it be known that he was ready for all-out war over the Gavia.

The stage began in the valley below Chiesa Valmalenco, under a chilling, butt-freezing rain. The peloton, led by the Bongos, who had

Coppino (Franco Chioccioli . . . the spitting image of Fausto Coppi) in pink, reluctantly left town. Lacking its usual chewable aggression, but full of fear, it headed into the Dolomites.

The first obstacle was Passo dell'Aprica, after 70 kilometers, at 4,000 feet. As we passed this summit en masse, the rain gave way to snow that was already sticking to the road. Except for Ariostea's resident brain surgeon, Stephan Joho, who was off the front, the boys were content to stay in the relative shelter of the peloton for as long as possible. The descent of the Aprica was rather scary for me, as my frozen-solid hands could not work the brakes. I was kind of slidin' the corners and rammin' into bikers in order to slow down.

As the descent leveled off, Roberto Pagnin broke away, gaining only a few seconds, as Del Bongo began their team time trial to the base of the Gavia. Ouch! My legs felt like petrified wood as we passed Ponte en Legno, the last outpost before the Gavia. Then, as each climber and G.C. man moved to the front, we passed the sign for the KoM—28 bloody k's. Umm, um, um, yummy.

Normally, at this point, I would drift back to the sprinters' *gruppetto* and hang as best I could to make the time limit. I sprinted up to Andy one last time with his rain jacket from the team car. I handed off his jacket and said, "Good luck, baby doll—give 'em the stick!" When I finally drifted back to the team car, Mike was visibly agitated, which is rare and made me instantly nervous. He stated yellin' about a blizzard on top of the pass and handed me some ski gloves, wool hat, and dry jacket and said, "Take this back up to Andy!" "Shit," I said. "Are you joking?" "Hell no! Get back up there with Andy's gear ASAP!" I shook my head and gritted my teeth and began closing in on the lead group. It took me 5 kilometers, but I finally caught Andy, Breuk, Giovannetti, and Giupponi. I yelled at Andy, "Take this shit. There's a blizzard on the pass."

The Day the Big Men Cried

Andy seemed surprised to see me at the front after 10 kilometers of climbing and just looked at me as if I were from Mars. As I drifted off the leaders, I caught a glimpse about two switchbacks ahead of the *maglia ciclamino* going solo and flying—until it disappeared, along with its wearer, Johan Van de Velde, into the now heavily falling snow. I also saw many of the fancied G.C. stars in various stages of distress. Slim Zim was suffering, and Coppino was downright pitiful. Visentini was ready to quit and Delgado had just decided that this Giro was going to be no more than Tour prep.

Besides the length, steepness, and elevation (almost 9,000 feet), what sets the Gavia apart is that the last 15 kilometers are not paved! If you have dry weather, the dust is choking . . . but in the rain and snow, all your force is lost just staying upright, as your tires sink into the mud. Even with 10 kilometers still to climb, the muddy trail became more and more snow packed. I kept pounding along—mostly solo, but occasionally passing the snow-covered remnant of a cycling icon. With 3 kilometers to the summit, there was a tunnel that offered some relief from the falling snow. I shook off some of the accumulated snow from my cotton cap, and took a cup of hot tea from one of the only tifosi I saw on the whole climb.

At the front, Andy was hanging mega tough with Breuk. They were about two minutes behind Van de Velde, who won the KoM. I went over the pass in the top 20, and Och', who was at the summit with our rain bags, went bonkers when he saw Big Bad Bobke dying hard and hanging with the climbers. I grabbed a plastic hat, long-finger gloves, and Oakley Pilots and took off down the pass for Bormio, a mere 15 kilometers away. I thought I could ride 15 downhill kilometers in any condition, at any time, anywhere on Earth. I have never been more wrong in my life.

After a brilliant climb, Van de Velde, forsaking extra clothes in order to gain time on the descent, was the leader on the road and had the pink jersey waiting for him in Bormio. Only 2 kilometers of descending later, Van de Velde was on his knees in tears. Savagely hypothermic, he crawled into a car to warm up. One hour later, he got out of the car and rode to the finish way outside the time limit. That left Drew and Breuk battling in front. . . .

All across Europe, news of the brutal conditions spread like a virus. The whole continent was glued to the TV, as Andy and Breuk duked it out for the stage win in the most abominable conditions ever. Breuk had that tiny bit extra and won the stage a second or so ahead of Andy. However, to the absolute astonishment of every man, woman, and child in Europe, an American team had the pink jersey. Andrew Hampsten climbed the highest step of the awards platform and donned *La Maglia Rosa*.

☆   ☆   ☆

After only 1 kilometer, I was bloody cold. After 2 kilometers, I was frozen to the core. After only 3 kilometers, I was laughing like a lunatic and screaming at the top of my lungs in an attempt to generate some warmth.

Meanwhile, I kept my head down and hammered, following the tire grooves through the snow. After only 1 kilometer, I was bloody cold. After 2 kilometers, I was frozen to the core. After only 3 kilometers, I was laughing like a lunatic and passed Rolf Sørensen, screaming at the top of my lungs in an attempt to generate some warmth. After 5 kilometers, I was crying and about to slip into a frozen coma. About halfway down, I was not thinking straight and was making poor choices. At one point, I got off my bike and began to run back up the hill in a lame attempt to warm up.

When Massimo Ghirotto came blastin' around a blind corner and barely missed T-boning me, I regained what little sense I had left. I jumped back on my bike and glued my eyes to Ghirotto's rear derailleur.

The Day the Big Men Cried

I actually had to fight just to stay in my body and remain conscious for the last 5 kilometers into Bormio.

There, I hit the finish line and collapsed. I was blue. My eyes were open, but I couldn't see. I screamed for Max—even though he was under my arm holding me up. Then I went out, 100 percent blackout. I began to regain my consciousness and my vision in the TV trailer set up next to the finish. When I came to, Max was in a panic, pounding on my chest, trying to jump start my heart.

The whole Giro entourage was madly running around the room, pouring hot coffee down the throats of 20 to 30 sides of frozen beef, all of us naked and blue as Paul Bunyan's ox. I regained enough composure to wrap up in a blanket and be driven to the hotel, only 100 meters from the finish. There, I sat in the hot shower for 50 minutes, but was still shaking from the cold. I jumped out of the shower to dive under a two-foot thick comforter . . . and was stopped in my tracks by Andy's beaming face with the pink jersey laying on top of his covers. "Whoa, baby, you look like an angel," I said.

At dinner that evening all of us—Wook, Raul, Pepe, D-Man, and Dag Otto—recapped the day. Of course, we all knew that defending the leader's jersey for the remaining week of racing would be harder than anything we had ever done. But as we stuffed ourselves with *pizzoccheri*, Torriani, the race director, came into the restaurant with a crisp-clean, brand new maglia rosa. Ohhhh yes!

The day of the Gavia was a race the cycling world had never seen. The favorites all had lost preposterous amounts of time. Zimmermann and Chioccioli both lost over five minutes; the 1986 Giro winner, Visentini, lost half an hour; G. Saronni lost almost an hour. In fact, the conditions were so extraordinary that even though almost half the field missed the time limit, any racer who finished was allowed to continue. The morning after the stage, *La Gazzetta* ran the headline, "The day the big men cried," and they were absolutely right.

LIST OF CHARACTERS

Drew = Andrew Hampsten

Bongos = the Del Tongo team

Coppino = Franco Chioccioli = means "little Coppi" after Fausto Coppi

Mike = Mike Neel

Och' = Jim Ochowicz

Max = Massimo Testa, 7-Eleven team doctor

Breuk = Erik Breukink

Maglia ciclamino = Points leader's purple jersey

Slim Zim = Urs Zimmermann

Wook = Ron Kiefel

D-Man = Davis Phinney

Raul = Raúl Alcalá

Pepe = Jeff Pierce

Dag Otto = Dag Otto Lauritzen

Torriani = Vincenza Torriani, Giro race director

pizzoccheri = Bormese specialty pasta

tifosi = Rabid cycling fans of Europe

La Gazzetta = *La Gazzetta della Sport*, Italy's daily sports newspaper

CHAPTER 3

One Racer's View

Tour de France

The Tour. Not the Vuelta a España. Not the Giro d'Italia. But the Tour. The Tour de France is it. The Tour is the pinnacle of the sport. The prestige, mystique, attention, and economic importance of the Tour make it the biggest sports happening of the year.

Where the Giro is beautiful,

The Tour is brutal.

Where the Vuelta is wonderful,

The Tour is wicked. . . .

In fact, the Tour is the crowning jewel of all cycling endeavors— whether that be commuting to work, a category-B criterium in Oklahoma City, a kermesse at any Belgian town, the Olympic road race, the spring classics, or the world championships.

The Tour is simple to understand. It's the race of the common people. They can easily grasp the difficulties of the Tour—the neverending climbs, the colorful speed of the peloton, the inherent danger of descending a mountain road at 100 kph. They can identify with the man in the yellow jersey . . . and the rider who drops behind and abandons the Tour in tears. And they recognize that no person will ever go faster, more beautifully on a bicycle than in the Tour de France.

The geographic diversity of France is another reason why the Tour has achieved its magnificent image. France has the perfect shape and terrain for a three-week bicycle race. And the French people—who will even argue about a game of *pétanque* in the village square—have a tremendous love for competition.

That is why they respect the Tour—which is pure racing. In fact, every aspect of a Tour rider's life is competitive. Racing to breakfast, getting in the team cars and racing to the start, racing all day on the bike, then getting back in the team cars to race to the hotel, racing to the showers . . . the massage table . . . the dinner table . . . and finally sleep. The Tour is also a race for the entire entourage: from the casual spectator to the busy journalist, the photographer, the *soigneur*, the race official, and the team-car driver. . . . Not one member of the Tour's cast of thousands has an easy task.

Although racing well at the Tour means economic well-being for a rider, money is never a part of the competitive equation. The pure joy of winning a stage, and especially the yellow jersey, transcends the prizes, perks, and prestige that such a success bestows on an individual.

The Tour generally starts in the north of France and follows a cycle of stages with moderate climbs and terrible speed, leading to the first long time trial—when the G.C. race begins to manifest itself. Then we come to the climbs in the second phase: the Alps and the Pyrénées. These mountains have traditionally been the fiercest battlefields, where the G.C. race is played out. But with Greg LeMond's use of new technology for a stunning upset of Laurent Fignon on the final day of the 1989 Tour, the time trials have become as important as the mountain stages. More climbs follow before the rush to the last time trial and the final, exhilarating race into Paris.

After three weeks of real suffering, you climb the final hill near Versailles and catch a glimpse of the Eiffel Tower as you drop into the city.

One Racer's View

You race around the Place de la Concorde, up the Champs-Elysées, make a hard left in front of the Arc de Triomphe, and bomb down to the finish before a mass of humanity. If you're lucky, your wife or mom is waiting under the Arc. And if you're really lucky, you aren't on a team that celebrates at some strip bar, but you're on an American team that gets to eat at a Tex-Mex restaurant in Montparnasse.

Had I not ridden the Tour, I would feel my career as a racer would be incomplete. The Tour tests every aspect of your abilities as a cyclist. It tests your reserves, health, speed, endurance, climbing, descending, bike handling in the pack, time trialing, cool, patience, and class.

Winning the Tour has created great champions and world-renowned heroes, like Fausto Coppi, Jacques Anquetil, Eddy Merckx, Bernard Hinault, Greg LeMond, and Miguel Indurain. But it exacts such a heavy toll that for many racers, it has become their singular crowning accomplishment. Men such as Luis Ocaña, Lucien Van Impe, Stephen Roche, and Pedro Delgado went so hard to win the Tour that they were never again able to attain that level of excellence. Yes, it's hard to live up to the lofty expectations that are created by the Tour—a race that transcends the individual.

If riding your bicycle through the countryside on a fine summer's day were equivalent to a child's pretty drawing of a wildflower, then the Tour is a Sistine Chapel fresco painted by Michelangelo. Even though some great twentieth-century writers, such as Hemingway, have mentioned the Tour in their work, why haven't they been able to capture the essence of the Tour de France? Perhaps because they weren't racing in it. But I think, because it's so dynamic and the atmosphere so rarefied, it is impossible to grasp the greatness and grandeur of the Tour with words alone. Maybe someday, a combination of song, pictures, and words will do fair justice to the greatest of all sporting contests.

CHAPTER 4

Believe or Leave

The Tour Worker's Credo

In 1990, Bobke took part in his third Tour de France. In his first Tour, in 1986, he came in 63rd, 1:43:26 behind Greg LeMond. In 1987, gastroenteritis forced Roll to quit the race in the 11th stage. And in 1988, he had to pull out before the start, when he crashed warming up for that year's "prelude" stage—and was replaced on the 7-Eleven team by rookie Nathan Dahlberg. After team boss Jim Ochowicz passed him by in 1989, Roll was proud to return to the Tour de France arena in 1990. . . .

June 30, 1990

Prologue, Futuroscope, 6.3 km

Believe or perish—I made it, man. I made it into the Tour. I am fully stoked and jazzed and, in general, dipped in doo. I have been struggling since 1986 to get into this race and I feel vindicated by being selected. All right! Awesome!! Geez, what a circus. I thought because the soccer Mondiale was still going most media attention would be down in Italy, but the cycling woodwork squeaks—and out come the freaks for the Tour. I went all out in my prologue, 110 percent, and didn't come in last, so I'm pleased. Almost everyone used triathlete bars—and Thierry Marie slayed all. Only three more weeks of torture. . . .

Believe or Leave

July 1

Stage 1a, Futuroscope circuit, 140 km

Got up early due to the fact that we have two stages today. Our team's Swiss cook, Willie, fully styled the boomboys to an awesome breakfast of real pasta and omelets. So we blasted out of Futuroscope and the bikers are nervous. I mean tense, tight, and paranoid. So Steve Bauer took advantage of this, with Frans Maassen, Claudio Chiappucci, and Ronan Pensec, and the field sat up. The break had 10.5 minutes at the finish—and Steve had the yellow jersey! Whoa! I am fully dipped, head to toe!

Stage 1b, Futuroscope TTT, 48 km

Well, we had to defend the yellow jersey with 8 seconds to spare. And we did it! Against Buckler, Z, and Carrera—we beat them all! Awesome!! You can pick any superlative, but it wouldn't come near to describing how well we raced. Sean Yates was incredible as usual, and we got 6th, but mainly kept the yellow jersey. Whoa! Today we did the job, man.

July 2

Stage 3, Poitiers-Nantes, 233 km

Long, hard day defending the jersey. We wasted all futile attempts to break away and kept the jersey. The homeboys scored one for themselves today. There were numerous attacks right from the start, and the field split with Laurent Fignon and Charly Mottet in the back. The other favorites raged for the dangerous early move, and Andy Hampsten went into the next dangerous break. In the finale, Moreno Argentin got away and it started raining, so we all just sat in front to protect Steve and kept the jersey for another day. Our director, Noël Dejonckheere, couldn't say jack to me today for chillin' in the back, because he never saw me the whole race.

July 3

Stage 4, Nantes–Mont St. Michel, 203 km

Nice day and a bonus totally because we kept the jersey. All right!! I ate it heavily due to a bonehead standing in the road—as will happen more often than not in wonderful France. What happened is that Gianni Bugno swerved to avoid the wandering Frenchman, taking out my front wheel and causing me to crash. My bike flipped up in the air and hit Sean Kelly in the ear. I had some explaining to do when Kelly gave me shit the next day. Other than that, another good day for the homeheads. I was just b.s.-ing with Greg LeMond, and he said, "Hey, Bob, I saw you asking an Italian yesterday how many guys were in the break, and you had one finger up, and it looked like you were about to pound his face." Whoa, I thought to myself. Greg is watching what I do, and asking me about it the next day in the freaking Tour de France! Holy Cats! I don't even believe it!!

☆ ☆ ☆

Greg is watching what I do, and asking me about it the next day in the freaking Tour de France! Holy Cats!

July 4

Stage 5, Avranches-Rouen, 301 km

Three zero one kilometers, man. What a miserable bitch today. Thirty kilometers from the start, guess what? Rain. Yes, you guessed it. Anyway, we kept the jersey another day, but it was serious today. Gerrit Solleveld got away with 100 km to go and was tanking. We started rotating with about 80 km to go, and just kept working and working. Even though the jersey wasn't in real trouble, we had to reduce the deficit to about 5 minutes at the finish. Because we kept getting the most looney time splits, we were nervous. So it was only 4 minutes at the end—no worries. I was totally waterlogged at the finish, and sleepy and tired and just sort of melancholy. I guess I miss the sun.

Believe or Leave

July 5

Transfer day

Flew to Strasbourg with every biker on the planet. I hate flying and was scared the whole flight—as usual. This was no rest day, and I rode about two hours and survived another flight. I tried to act cool, but I was a basket case of nerves and just tried to forget the whole Tour thing for one day—the yellow jersey, the bonus sprints, the counterattacks and attacks and tempo, and the whole Tour pressure media circus, the go-till-you-blow type of lifestyle we have for the summer of our glorious youths. So the Tour is not just a number of kilometers on a map per day. The Tour is the cat's meow, man. Meow!!

July 6

Stage 6, Sarrebourg-Vittel, 202.5 km

The boys delivered the goods today! We didn't talk, we didn't gossip, we didn't piss, or eat our paninis, or dream about sunny days in the good ol' USA. We died out in the wind to defend the yellow jersey—which we did for another day. The stage was nervous and windy, and I felt sluggish from my crash and the transfer day, but the stage went by pretty quickly. So now we've had the jersey for a good while, and everyone is getting totally jazzed. Like I said, believe or leave. Och' and Noël are like a pair of proud fathers, just grinning from ear to ear and happy about our job, which is very nice for the homeboys to see.

July 7

Stage 7, Vittel-Epinal TT, 61.5 km

Today is my birthday, and Steve gave me one beauty of a gift. He kept the yellow jersey! All right! Very hard, rolling course, and I felt pretty smooth. Usually I barely miss the time limit in TTs, but today I was pretty strong and smooth and just cruised, so I will be able to work harder in the next few days. That is the life of a worker. Even if you feel good, you must take care not to go too hard and get blown out. I don't mind being a worker, as long as I get some recognition for my work, and now we are getting loads of it, so no worries. Rául Alcalá lay waste to all, with his aero' tuck, big ol' butty, and heart the size of Texas. We ate some cake for my 30th birthday, and they bought me a big card and all the bikers signed it, plus a guest: Eddy Merckx. Whoa! Who would have predicted that a sketchy short-order cook from Nor Cal would be eatin' cake with E. Merckx during the Tour de France. . . .

July 8

Stage 8, Epinal-Besançon, 181.5 km

More rain and rain and rain. I am almost at my rain limit, I swear. I think all the bikers were tired today, so the race didn't really get rolling until the finale. There were some pretty decent hills at the end, but no worries. Ron "Wookie" Kiefel got in a break, and too bad all the sprinters were in the break. So Wook got third and Olaf Ludwig wasted all—surprise, surprise. We still have the jersey, which is great, and makes the bad weather not as bad as it could be.

July 9

Stage 9, Besançon-Geneva, 196 km

Killer up-and-down stage. We also had a very difficult chase to take back a dangerous break with Maassen. I didn't feel too great, but once we started to rotate in the front, I felt much better. We finally caught the break after about 30 km of chasing—right at the bottom of a second-category hill—and me, Sean, Norm Alvis, and Davis Phinney got shelled directly. But we kept the jersey another day. Tomorrow, the Tour de France starts for real. I am totally hammered by working all week and sweating out the yellow-jersey pressure. I feel strong enough, but I am still nervous before the Alps . . . as usual.

July 10

Stage 10, Geneva–St. Gervais, 119 km

Well, finally we had a nice day with the weather. This stage, being so short, was direct into the big passes. First, we did a first category hill, the Col de la Colombière. It was hard, and split the race way up. Then, down that and immediately the Col des Aravis, which wasn't too bad. Then we went up some gnarly goat path near Mont Blanc. Whoa, that was 8 kilometers— steep! Pensec rode really well and got the jersey. However, there's a long way to go.

July 11

Stage II, St. Gervais–L'Alpe de Huez, 182 km

Now we're in the Tour de France. Today was a monster mountain stage. For breakfast: the Col de la Madeleine, 25 km of steep, long, hard torture. For lunch, Lord have Mercy: the Col du Glandon. Oh man, that was 17 km of abject suffering. The last 4.5 kilometers are back-breaking, steep, leg-breakers. Then, for your humble supper: a big slice of Alpe d'Huez pie. Our whole team was in the main field here—with Andy riding great up front and Davis doing a long solo behind. I felt pretty good and went at my tempo, and I still felt totally hammered. One thing about today that was absolutely great was the number of U.S. fans on L'Alpe d'Huez. Hearing Americans cheering for us was really nice. Only one more day in the Alps . . . and I'm still here.

July 12

Stage 12, Fontaine–Villard de Lans TT, 34 km

Felt pretty good today, not great, but I went at a hard tempo and finished okay. The race went right up a hill for 11 km, and that was not so easy. Then it was rolling for a while, and the last 3 kilometers were quite steep.

Pensec blew and Chiappucci took the jersey. That shirt is one heavy load, bro'.

Really starting to lose my mind, as will happen in the Tour. My chain slipped off just before my start and a spectator came over to help me put it back on. I thought if anyone touched my bike it would just blow up and fall into pieces, so I was screaming for this guy to get away from my bike. I was about to miss my start, when the team mechanic came over to help me. My mind is really turning to Tour de France mush.

July 13

Rest day

Today was the rest day and that is exactly what I did. I had a fever last night, so I felt weak and just slept all day. As a bonus, this is the worst hotel of the entire Tour. And we get to stay here for two nights. Oh, I love France.

We are staying with the PDM and Weinmann teams, and all the wives and girlfriends have shown up as usual. Plus, about ten television stations, and fifty reporters, plus hundreds of bike fans. What you get is Ringling Bros. Circus, not a freaking rest day. The only peace you get is going for a bike ride. Isn't that special?

July 14

Stage 13, Villard de Lans–St. Étienne, 149 km

Bastille Day. We came out of the mountains and down into the furnace of central France. Whoa, the race exploded on a relatively gentle terrain profile. But the heat was such a shock, the field just detonated in about ten groups, and Chiappucci lost almost 5 minutes to the first group, and Pensec lost over 7. Andy rode great and got 3rd. This here stage was the real Tour, where you get in the gutter from the start and stay there, groveling on the wheel in front of you the whole day . . . ouch! Today, each kilometer seemed to take about an hour. Paris seems years away, and I can't even remember the team time trial. Where am I, anyway?

July 15

Stage 14, Le Puy–Millau, 205 km

I was absolutely dead meat for 100 km of this stage. I could barely sit on the wheels. We all really suffered today. Now we are deep into the Tour. We are all full of the beautiful and hideous Tour delirium. It was another scorcher today, and we had four hills right at the start, then rolling terrain, then a steep category-two hill, before a long descent into Millau. Bugno's Chateau d'Ax boys started a chase from 60 km to go, and we flew all the way to Millau. Each kilometer, it got hotter and hotter. All the groups came together at the bottom of the last hill, with 5 kilometers to go, and Marino Lejarreta just blasted off the front to win alone. I think the whole peloton suffered like dogs today.

July 16

Stage 15, Millau-Revel, 170 km

Oh Lord, now it is hot!! Today was another hideous day of hell in the boiling French sun. I got overheated in the finale and sat up with 8 kilometers to go—no way. Many guys got blown out today in the heat. Mottet just took off and killed everyone.

Today, I was sitting at the Bollé booth for publicity for our sunglass sponsor in the village départ, as usual. And all the people came up to ask for glasses. Geez, it was embarrassing. I think if you give away free stuff, people turn into shameless beggars. Gawddd, it was embarrassing. What a circus.

July 17

Stage 16, Blagnac–Luz Ardiden, 215 km

Into the wicked Pyrénées. Today was sort of weird, because everyone was totally wasted and we had like 140 km of flat before the climbs. So everyone went S-L-O-W. I mean piano. I have never seen slow like that in the Tour. Of course, on the first hill, the Col d'Aspin, everyone went beserk full out. Ouch, I suffered on the first hill and was way off the back. I chased and caught up to the main field, and went up the Tourmalet. Whoa! That is one gnarly hill. But I felt a little better and hung in there. Then we went down the Tourmalet at terminal velocity and straight up Luz-Ardiden, and I felt pretty good to survive such a desperate day. LeMond had his finest hour and came within 5 seconds of Chiappucci. Greg is looking like the winner of this year's TdF, for real.

July 18

Stage 17, Lourdes-Pau, 150 km

Lourdes is a bizarre place. It's a sort of Kmart for Catholics, and provided a weird takeoff point for this final mountain stage.

Only 10 km down the road was the Col d'Aubisque. I mean this is a 30-kilometer hill. Geez, that means we will be climbing for the next 2 hours. Ouch. That's no joke. Thank God, the bikers went at a steady tempo, and I felt pretty good and hung in the front of the group, and we all went screaming down the Aubisque and straight up the Marie Blanque. Whoa, the race blew to pieces. LeMond flatted near the top of the Marie Blanque and all hell broke loose. Z had to call two guys back from the break to work, and they all came back. But the tempo was frantic for all groups. Anyway, our whole team is still intact, thanks to Willie, our chef.

Believe or Leave

July 19

Stage 18, Pau-Bordeaux, 212 km

Hot! Today was so hot and the Pyrénées were so hard, it was nice that the pack went slow for about 140 km. Then Phil Anderson went for it like a full-blown bat straight out of hell! And the speed went from about 25 kph to 60 kph, in the space of 500 meters. I swear to God, that was painful. We never went less than 55 kph to the finish, and Bugno just went flying off the front. Whoa, I was fully dipped. I could hardly believe my eyes. I'd say about one-third of the bikers had heat prostration today, and that is no fun at all. Davis was out of it. His head looked like a red water balloon about to explode. So I gave him some help as he was about to be dropped. He hung tough, though, and finished in the bunch, despite a pile of bikers getting shelled by the wicked tempo and insane heat.

July 20

Stage 19, Castillon la Bataille–Limoges, 182.5 km

The last 14 days have been the most unforgiving, unrelenting heat I have ever felt. Not just the days, but the nights are so hot that you can't sleep. And today I was really feeling the effects. I was moody and bummed out, and nervous and all that TdF psycho paranoia. So we get to the start after a long drive, and I roll out of the car and stroll to sign on. The announcer calls me over. I'm like unshaved, skinny, wearing a full frown, and it turns out that I won the daily Grand Prix Performance for the guy who moved up the most on G.C. the previous stage. Whoa! I started jumping up and down. I couldn't believe it when all the photographers came up and started snapping photos while I got my trophy and flowers, and all that good trash. You've got to believe, or you're dead meat. Noël had the gall to say, "Some guys have all the luck." Shit, I worked my balls off for this.

July 21

Stage 20, Lac de Vassivière TT, 45.5 km

Another hot one—I went mellow and survived. LeMond pulled out every stop possible and creamed Chiappucci to take over the yellow jersey. Chiappucci really raced well the last week to keep the jersey, so in Italy I hope the rabid tifosi are placated. But LeMond was way too good and strong, and would have done whatever was necessary to win this race the past three weeks. Our team finished 3rd on team today, which is very good. Dag-Otto Lauritzen was the leading rider for almost the whole race, and finished 5th on the stage, which was great! So tomorrow is Paris and the Champs-Elysées.

I feel like Steve McQueen's Papillon on Devil's Island: "I'm still here, you bastards."

July 22

Stage 21, Bretigny sur Orge–Paris, 183 km

Whoa, dude. I just finished the Tour de France! Superlatives fade when you climb the last hill near Versailles and descend into Paris and see the Eiffel Tower and cruise around the Place de la Concorde and turn up the Champs Elysées and see the Arc de Triomphe. I can't tell you, but I got chills and goose bumps. After three weeks of all-out racing that

☆   ☆   ☆

After three weeks of all-out racing that makes you really wonder about what in hell you are doing with your life, you find a reason to believe.

makes you really wonder about what in hell you are doing with your life, you find a reason to believe. After chasing the wheels and dodging crashes and crawling up mountains and screaming down them, seeing the finish banner is an incredible experience. Like I said: Death to disbelievers!

July 23

Boxmeer, Netherlands, 100 km epilogue

By an act of pure insanity, I signed up to do four criteriums here in the Netherlands. I was totally wasted tonight, and these guys really race! The crit started at 8 p.m., and we did 40 laps of a 2.2-km circuit, and it was fast. I could barely sit on the wheel. These crits are designed for the Dutch people to get a chance to see their Tour heroes in the flesh, and give the racers a chance to make some money. The problem for me is that they start the next dang day after the Tour. The Tour sort of envelops your whole life. Whoa, stop this train. See you tomorrow night.

☆　☆　☆

Bobke finished his third Tour de France in 132nd place, 2 hours, 14 minutes, 50 seconds behind LeMond. The 7-Eleven rider's team leaders, Hampsten and Bauer, finished 11th and 27th, respectively. The team, which finished all of its riders, came in 9th of the 22 squads in the team competition.

Blind Faith
was My Motto
at the '86 Tour

I have heard faith can move mountains, but I know, for sure, it can get an ex-East Bay lowrider through the Tour de France.

During the spring classic season of 1986, in Europe, all of us on the 7-Eleven team suffered like dogs. The races were as fast and hard as always . . . the weather was particularly nasty . . . and 1986 was our first full-blown campaign in Europe as a professional cycling team. Because of these factors—and some conflicting personalities within the team—we basically looked like sheer shit. Consequently, the management began to have second thoughts about accepting the first Tour de France invitation for any American squad.

Alexi Grewal, our team leader, brought things to a head one day during one of the nastiest, most wicked races of the whole year—the Three days of De Panne, on Belgium's North Sea coast.

Our soigneur, Shelly Verses, had made arrangements for us to suit up and relax at a local café before another day of dying in the gutter—while seeking shelter from the crosswind in Flanders. And so we were suiting up, looking at each other, shaking our heads, when a school group of retarded people all filed into the café . . . as they probably had been doing since World War I. Alexi went bonkers, saying, "I have got to get out of here. . . ." I said, "Whoa, Flex," but he was long gone out the door. Meeting him as he was storming out of the café was a reporter the Belgian paper *Het Volk* had sent to ask us how we were doing in beautiful Belgium. Suffice it to say, it wasn't a pretty scene, and the next day, the sports page had a giant picture of Alexi—with a fat, 7-Eleven sticker on his beanie and a huge headline: "I piss on Belgium." Och' flew over direct; and after he saw us all get shelled and drop out of the Flèche Wallonne, he called a meeting.

We were scheduled to do the Vuelta a España, and Och' said if we didn't win a stage there, we weren't going to the Tour de France. I looked around the room at the faces of the boys . . . and I saw mostly a look of relief. Except for Wookie. Wook started grinding his teeth, and his eyes narrowed and took on the clear, cold color of steel. As I watched his resolve wash away the weariness that had seeped into his bones, I jumped up and yelled, "Let's kill them Spanish bastards!" Everyone laughed, but I was serious. I'm not sure if, at that point, any of us were capable of winning a stage in that Vuelta; but as it turned out, we didn't have to.

We arrived at Palma, Majorca, a resort island in the Mediterranean, for the start of the Vuelta, five days early. Three days before the prologue, hundreds of fighter jets began screaming across the sky—all day and into the night. We all knew that somewhere, some serious shit was going down. Sure enough, President Ron Ray-gun had decided he didn't like Muammar el-Qaddafi's face, and figured he better bomb the crap out of schools and hospitals in Libya. The management decided we better get the hell out of the middle of the Mediterranean Sea and back to the sweet land of milk, honey, and missile silos. Consequently, our Tour de France preparation consisted of Mexico's Tour of Baja and the Redlands Classic in Southern California, instead of the Vuelta a España. And not only did we win a stage at Redlands, we won about all the stages. So the management figured we were ready for the Tour de France. . . .

The 1986 Tour was the most difficult, challenging, and plain brutal race I have ever done: seventy-seven categorized climbs, and a horrible duel between Greg LeMond and Bernie Hinault, made it netherworldly hard. And the first 10 days were so insanely fast, they eventually forced almost eighty of the world's best pros to drop out. I desperately did not want to quit, but after 10 days of barely hanging onto the wheels for dear life, I got violently ill. And I won't soon forget that night—which we spent in a gymnasium, sleeping on cots with nine other teams. As I lay down to sleep, vomit exploded from my stomach, and I barely made it to the trash can in the corner. Running across the gym, jumping over cots full of sleeping bikers, made for a rugged, exhausting night, as every poison-laden fluid in my body exited at the nearest orifice.

The next day, I was wrung out, utterly wasted. I spent 100 km glued to Alain Bondue's wheel—dead-last in a line of 200 guys going 60 kph, single-file—dying, and praying not to die. Finally, I couldn't sit on the wheel anymore, and got dropped. I bit back hard on desperate tears, realizing I could never make the time limit, since we had another 160 km to go to the finish. The caravan of follow cars all passed me, and as the last team car went past, I was about to weep . . . when the peloton miraculously sat up. My heart leapt for joy as I caught up, and I knew if I could hang on for a while, I could make the time limit. When I finished the stage with the peloton, the boys who slept in the gym the night before absolutely could not believe I was still in the race.

The next three stages were merciless, inhumanly hard days in the Pyrénées and into the oven of central France. The sun had turned the chip-and-seal roads to playdough, and—kick me hard in the balls—I got sick again. The walls of my hotel room bled as hallucinations replaced sleep—

interrupted only by screaming voices ringing in my head as I ran to the toilet to vomit. This time, I was in tears before the day's stage even started. I packed my bags, made plane reservations, and told Shelley V. to drive me to the airport from the first feed zone.

When that day's stage started, we went easy for about 10 meters, until some moron launched, and we all were in single file going 60 kph. I couldn't believe it. You can't even drop out of the Tour easily. I dug down deep and somehow managed to stay in the pack, until we reached the first feed zone. When Shelley saw me coming, she naturally held out the feed bag. I looked at her funny, but grabbed my bag and kept going. The moment I reached for that feed, I changed. From then on, I wanted to finish the Tour de France.

Since I hadn't slept or eaten in two days, I was famished after the stage and ate a huge dinner with a gigantic peach melba for dessert. The next day, I woke up—after actually sleeping—and ate four ham-and-cheese omelets. While this eating took the edge off my appetite, I became as constipated as the Colorado River at Hoover Dam.

When we started the next stage, I had about 7 pounds of manure in my bowels. After carrying half my body weight in my lower intestines for three hours into the stage, the load decided to cut loose. Sheeeeeiittt! I desperately grabbed my jersey, trying to pull it off right in the middle of the peloton. I got it over my head . . . and it stuck right there. Mike Neel had pinned my number on that day—through my jersey, through my T-shirt, and into my bib shorts, I was as blind as a bat weaving through the pack, spastically yanking on my jersey and knocking Colombians and Spaniards over like bowling pins. Finally, the road curved and I went straight . . . straight into a ditch. I was careening down the ditch spraying mud on all the spectators, until finally I smashed into a driveway and went flying over the bars in a blind somersault, tearing loose the jersey.

I left the bike right there, ducked behind a tall hedge, and squatted down for a massive doo.

Meanwhile, Mike is driving along in the caravan and sees my bike lying in a driveway in bumpuke France. He stops and asks where in freaking French hell is the guy who was riding it. The spectators started yelling at Mike, because I had covered them all in mud, so Mike starts screaming, "Bob, where the hell are you?" I figured I better finish and get going. So I look around for some leaves, and instead, find a family of absolutely horrified French people staring at me from the picnic they were having on their front lawn. They looked at me in utter disbelief and exasperation as I smiled, grabbed a linen napkin, wiped myself, grabbed a piece of cake, and ran in a full, Carl Lewis sprint. Mike was on the road, shaking his head in pure wonder, and I said, "When you got to go man, you got to go." I hung tough the rest of the stage, and the rest of the Tour. . . .

People frequently ask me, "What is the Tour like?" It is always difficult to explain, but if you mix pure torture and exquisite pleasure with a ton of faith, you will get a good idea.

☆　☆　☆

Bob Roll finished 63rd out of 131 finishers in the 1986 Tour de France.

Springtime in Hell

A New Season, a New Sponsor

January 3, 1991

Hooeyyy!!! Just signed a one-year contract with the Motorola Cycling Team! Lord have mercy. I'd been sitting around at Doom's Gate looking down both barrels of poverty since August 10, when I got a letter from the Club (7-Eleven Cycling Team). I was out of work. Suffice it to say, since then I've been seriously frowning. But the rattling death train I've been so seriously conducting just got derailed by a thin fax from Motorola. All twisted Euro' dogs tighten down your boot straps—Bobke's back!!!

January 13

Flying to Chicago for Motorola Corporation introduction and media program. I do not like getting on planes. I don't mind flying, but crashing bugs me. So I get off the plane, and there is a guy in a Motorola jacket, and before I even open my mouth he says, "Mr. Roll?" I say, "Hi," and we stroll. We pick up Ron "Wookie" Kiefel and Scott McKinley at the next gate. Then we go to Phil Anderson's gate. The gate opens and this rock group, the Black Crowes, gets off the plane and stands right in the way, so everyone has to walk around them. I say, "Hey, you boneheads, wanna quit blocking the door?" They all turned to look at me and saw four stone age cavemen . . . and moved. Then the missing link, Anderson, gets off the plane and the Black Crowes sit down. Norm Alvis smiles behind his shades and says to me, "You're crazy, aren't you?" We split for Schaumburg, Illinois. We pass the world's largest mall, and slot into the Hyatt. Yesterday, I was high in the Rocky Mountains, straddling the Continental Divide—the snow under my left foot would give birth to the denizens of the Pacific deep; the snow under my right would feed Atlantic leviathans. And today, I'm squatting smack dab in the middle of industrial America. The snow under my feet won't give birth to jack shit . . . whoa! Biking for cash is strange, bro'.

January 14

Took a long, strange tour of the Motorola facility. We had a huge banquet at the Motorola museum, with a big pile of bigwigs. I wanted to make a favorable impression on the head honcho whom they sat me next to, so I didn't say jack.

January 15

After a rough flight out to our California training camp in Santa Rosa, I was greeted at the airport in San Francisco by my beautiful, Irish-American mom. I arranged for her to pick me up so we could catch up on family business on the drive to Santa Rosa, since I've been AWOL since 1982. I'm glad she picked me up, because the team van got lost somewhere in San Francisco and ended up on Castro Street, dependent on directions from men all dressed in black leather who were very excited to see a van full of youth athletes with shaved legs.

January 16

Niiiiice, sunny day, and we're finally back on our bicycles. Felt good to be surrounded by my homeboys, cool breezin' down the Pacific coast. Went to a Mexican restaurant with practically the whole team, because most of them come from places where tamales are as rare as the April sun in Flanders.

January 17

Another nice day, soft pedaling through redwood forests out to the coast. Rode about 6 hours; not feeling too bad. Saw some massive birds of prey, who gracefully demonstrate this world's maximum evolution.

January 18

Ooohhh! Long, hilly 6-hour ride and I blew savage, sky-high chunks. I copped a wicked bonk on the last hill and barely crawled back to the hotel. I also crashed on this way-slick piece of pavement and took down Dag-Otto Lauritzen. Mike Carter crashed on top of me—but I didn't even notice, he's so light. Only moments before I crashed, a truck passed us; and if the driver had finished his last sip of coffee, we'd all be fish food.

January 19

Since I felt so lame yesterday, I took an easy, three-hour ride today. Then watched good cartoons and bad movies all day at the crib.

January 20

That's better, bro'—8 hours on Skaggs Road to the coast. Skaggs is this old logging road, recently paved, with nothing but hills and curves and descents. After about 4 hours on this road, you go up this steep hill and get all delirious, because Phil and Mike were having a pulling duel at the front.

January 21

Big Penance Day for the annual photo shoot. We all take individual photos and millions of team photos, until you absorb so much radiation from the flashes that you look like the Swamp Thing. So afterward I wanted to spin out my legs for a couple of hours. This year, I'm trying to train with smaller gears in the hope of smoothing out my pedaling style. But so far it doesn't matter, because I couldn't push a gear even if I paid the gear gods a million clams.

January 22

At our usual morning meeting, our boss, Sheila Griffin, came from Motorola. I was hiding out in my silent corner—as usual, when sponsors show—until she circulated a letter that she received last November. Seems that an army colonel stationed in Amman, Jordan, was pleased that Motorola is sponsoring a pro bike team, et cetera. He had some suggestions for Motorola, and when Sheila read suggestion No. 3, everyone went bonkers: "Number three—Hire Bob Roll!!!" I almost fell off my seat. Whoa, I jumped up and started doing the Bobke Strut around the room, getting "high fives" from all the homeboys. I was flying. Dag-Otto was absolutely convinced I either paid the Army colonel, or he was a relative. I've got to get fit and kick some serious ass!!

January 23

Mondo, 9-hour ride way up to Clear Lake with homeheads Wookie, Phil, Nate Dahlberg, Sean Yates, Steve Bauer, and Brian "Brain" Walton. They all turned around at Clear Lake, but I kept going west by myself. I wanted to do a *long* ride, so I had to climb over toward the coast to Cloverdale. A brush fire was burning on this long climb, and I had to dodge the fire marshal to continue on my epic. As I climbed, the wind shifted and blew the smoke out of my path and I passed the fire, no problem. I kept going, and as the hours went by, I felt stronger and stronger until I was flying down the road. Before I got back to the hotel, the sun went down, and I was nervous about stacking into some unseen hole. But I made it back safe and consumed massive amounts of bovine flesh.

Springtime in Hell

January 25

Seven hour, semi epic with John Tomac. Rode out of town on a hard hill along Kings Ridge Road. Ouch! Then we turned north into the Himalayas past this Buddhist temple—out in the boonies—with brass dome roofs and millions of flags out in the wind. Directly after that, we passed a huge pig farm, with tons of manure all over the road. I love Northern Cal, man. At the moment, the team has been wiped out by this virus; but me, Norm, and Scott haven't got it, so I figure it must be a California virus that people from all over the planet get when they come here, begin to pile on miles, and eat tons of Mexican food. Eeee . . . holy frijole!

January 26

The camp is breaking up, and me and Nate are the only ones left. So we rode for about 5 hours, then I drove him to San Jose for his flight to Wanganui, New Zealand. Geez, all I have to do is drive to San Francisco.

TOUR OF SICILY
February 22

I rode my bike for 3 hours around Palermo, Italy, today. I am in a state of complete culture shock. There are cars to dodge, and people and buses and motor scooters and rabid dogs. The people are packed in here so tight, compared to where I just came from, that I can hardly breathe.

February 23

Stage 1, Tour of Sicily

I survived today just enough to tell the tale. We started slow and easy, and I didn't feel too bad. Then, on the descent, a break got away and went up to 4 minutes directly. So the last 70 km, they chased the break like banshees. I was hanging on for dear life. Abdo-something-or-other from

Carrera won the stage, and Phil got a bitchin' second in a gnarly head-wind field sprint. The dude must be raging. He just won the Tour of the Med like the others were in some other race. So we are all pretty stoked. Tomorrow, however, is a serious stage. Where are my legs?!!

February 24

Ohhh man, a hard day—220 km with a few good hills, then a wicked circuit at the end. I did a truckload of work today—getting bottles, flatted, chasing after Phil, getting food, and chasing a Spanish guy who had an 8-minute lead on the peloton. Plus this ONCE rider stacked it face first right in front of me, going about 80 kph on a long descent. I swear my heart was beating fast enough already. So we get to the circuit and I flat, then I bonk so hard that I am cross-eyed and ride it in—before the sun went down, at least. The boys rode to the hotel, but I was too wasted to even untie my shoes.

February 25

Up to Modica for stage 3—this is the cradle of Western Civilization? Geez, what a place. I think they ran out of natural resources here about a million years ago, so they built this town out of human bones, and this cloud hangs over the city like some evil shroud. We do a long, hard race to get here, then shred five circuits with a nasty hill and descent each lap. I say to myself, If I crash here, and get those nasty germs under my skin, I'll get a fever so hideous I'll melt straight into the Earth. So I took no chances and survived another day. Maurizio "Mau Mau" Fondriest snagged the stage and made it out of town alive. We should all be so lucky.

February 26

Piano, piano—not *pianoforte*, man, I mean P-I-A-N-O. Nobody can go slow like Italians when the sun is out. Nobody. We all noodled down the coast to

Messina, where some plague entered Europe some million years ago and wiped out about 85 percent of the population, so the remaining 15 percent built a bunch of monuments dedicated to the plague. Now I'm suffering like a dog for these people's enjoyment. But not as much as Italian rider William Dazzani, who face-planted into the pavement, broke his jaw, shattered 12 teeth, and went straight into lala land with a concussion, oooooouchhhh! Biking for cash is so weird. Mario Cipollini walked away with the stage for the Del Bongo boys.

Then, after the stage, we drove across Sicily to the next hotel, where each and every team is staying. For some strange reason, we all ate way too much for dinner. So after dinner, me, Sean, and J.T. split for a hiking mission to this castle on top of the hill behind the hotel. We bushwhacked awhile, climbed some fences, and dodged some rabid dogs. Finally, we got to the castle and checked it out. On the way back, we walked past this house, and I sort of looked in the open front door, and an old, Italian woman was milking a cow—Whoa! Hold it right here, dudes, we got to check this out. So I say, "Hey, what the hell is a cow doing in your house, Mama Mia?"—not that it was any of my business. So I got the whole rundown on the milk-cow business of Sicily from the woman and her ancient husband. I told them that I'd come back tomorrow night with team hats, and we kept strollin' back to our hotel. The hotel was half a mile away, but this family had never been there. I swear I was fully dipped in milk-cow manure!

February 27

Fast, way-fast stage today, won again by Cipolla. I felt pretty good and finished in the front group—even though there were only about 50 guys left at the finish, due to the nasty hill we climbed three times in the finale. I was hammered afterward, but rode back to the hotel anyway and hit the sheets for a nap. J.T. has his personal stereo with most excellent speakers, and we blast D. Yoakam, J. Cash, W. Jennings, and many other white-trash outlaw heroes that Europeans have never heard of, so they understand that Madonna isn't the only singer from America. Anyway, after dinner, I got a couple of hats and started to walk up the hill to the milk farmers. I guess there isn't much hay in Sicily, so the promoters must collect the hay bales after each stage and use them again. So I "borrowed" one off the truck and carried it on my back up the hill for the cows. The family was out in front of the house after the evening milking. The old man was nervous about the hay, until I explained where I got it. They were happy to get some hats and all that trash, and gave me some fresh milk. I mean *fresh* from the cow.

February 28

Great balls o' fire! Phil just won the Tour of Sicily! The race blasted out of town, and I was coughing up parts of the breakfast I ate this morning. I am constantly amazed at the speed by which these lunkheads can propel their bicycles. Anyway, we had a mad dash for 70 km, leading to the first hill of the day, which was quite difficult. I went direct to the gruppetto, happy to have made it in one piece to the last day of this year's Tour of Sicily. Phil, however, was just beginning to rage. The peloton went over the hill chasing an early breakaway at full tilt. The breakaway was splitting up, and the peloton just exploded on the final circuit—due to hard hills, lots of corners, narrow streets, and a light rain that fell for only a few minutes, but made the road as slick as a greased sow. Phil shredded headlong into this mess and crossed the line, just as the last breakaway survivors were caught. He scored the time bonus for winning the stage, and had enough of a gap over Giuseppe Petito to win the race overall as well. So we were all celebrating around the team cars—all right!! Then, Noël calls on the C.B. and says I have to go to dope control as a random pick. So I stroll over there and sit down, after telling the UCI official I am there. As I wait, Petito comes in, totally bummed. He had been leading the race since day two and his team has been slaving every day like maniacs, because this is one of the most important Italian races. Then Max Sciandri from Carrera comes in trying to explain to the press how Phil got away at the last possible minute to win the whole bowl of chili. Then Phil comes in and says, "Hey Bobke, what d'ya think of that?" I told him that I was stoked and all that good trash. As soon as I got back to the hotel, Phil and Sean split for Het Volk in Belgium, leaving the Italians to eat bitter pasta indeed.

A FRENCH 'CRITERIUM'
March 30

Stage 1, Critérium International, Avignon, France

Fast, whoa, we flew down the highway today. Soon after the start was an MG—French for Best Climber prime—and since Nate's wife Kerensa had their first baby this morning in New Zealand, Nate wanted to win this first sprint. So he asked me to lead him out. I said "No doubt." So we go ape and Nate takes the King of the Mountain sprint, no worries. After about 70 km, the pack starts motivating and for the final 100 km, all 200 guys were in one long, suffering line. I hung on by the skin of my teeth and finished in the main field. I was pleased, as many dudes got shelled out the back. Six guys got up the road and had 12 seconds at the end, and J-C. Leclercq of Helvetia won the stage. This almost albino Brit, Dave Rayner, was also in the break, and wound up 6th out of six. So, since he is new over here, Rayner better hope his director, Jan Raas, is in a generous mood. I explained to him that unless you win the race, it is better not to even go in the final breakaway. So I say to Dave, "Hey Rayner, Jan Raas is gonna kick your butt unless you win this race on G.C. after botching that sprint." He says, "Yeah, I know." Ain't bikin' grand?

March 31

Stage 2 and 3

Morning stage: Nothing but hills at full tilt this morning. I was hanging on for dear life right from the *départ.* Whoa, we were smoking out of town. After about 100 all-out kilometers, we went up a Cat. I climb and the race blew to shreds. I was doing okay in the second group, where I usually hang out during massive Euro' climbs, and not feeling too bad. Then we came back around and did the same hill again. Ouch! But I hung on. Now, only the first 60 guys on G.C. get to do the final TT this afternoon and about 30 guys were in the first group, so I figured I would probably be in there. That is good because I *hate* to drop out of races. I'd rather have my fingernails burned off slowly than drop out of a Euro' pro race. Then, I sort of noodled off the front of my group to do some clowning around in the final 5 km to the finish. Except I look back and here comes Thomas Wegmüller *full* blast with Dean Woods and Louis De Koning. Geez! So I get on their wheels and we gain about a minute on the second group, so I'm in there for sure. Dave Rayner got shelled and I pity the next time he sees Raas. Charly Mottet slayed all to snag the leader's jersey.

Afternoon TT: Well, I went as hard as I could, and nobody caught me. The TT was dead flat for 12 km, and Wegmüller started 1 minute behind me. I figured if I could pedal 5 km before he caught me, I probably would do all right. But he never did, so I am pleased. My form is coming along pretty well, and the classics are about to begin up north. I was supposed to go home today, but Och' says, "Get in my car, we're going to Belgium." I say, all right!!

THREE DAYS OF DE PANNE
April 1

Back in Belgium. Drove all night to get here. Och' was on a mission, plus the Three Days of De Panne starts tomorrow, so we wanted to get up here

Springtime in Hell

ASAP. I cruise down to breakfast, and Yates sees me for the first time since the Tour of Sicily. Various stories about my premature death have been circulating, so Yates was jazzed to see Bobke back on the wheel.

April 2

Stage 1, Three Days of De Panne, 100 km

I felt pretty good today and stayed in the front, all the hills not withstanding. Phil launched on the third of five hills with Rolf Järmann of Weinmann, Sciandri of Carrera, and Johan Capiot of TVM. They got a good gap directly, and the pack had to shred in the finale, but the pack never took the break back. Max Sciandri won the sprint and Phil got 3rd. Phil is flying. If Phil had missed the break, we [Motorola] would have had to do the chase. I wouldn't mind actually doing a mondo chase with the homeboys, but our time will soon come, I'm sure.

Afternoon TT: Just when you thought it was safe to lie down in bed, you have to do a 20-km TT up and down around and about, and pray you don't get caught and look like a lame-o from America. I didn't get caught . . . but I didn't catch anyone either. Now I am wasted. I couldn't hardly get changed after my race, and after we drive back to Ghent, eat dinner, sleep—if we can—we get to do 240 km up nine cobbled hills of the Flemish Ardennes. Mister Wizard, helppp, ahhh. . . .

April 3

Stage 3, 240 km Kemmel, Taienberg, Patersberg, Berg Ten Houte, This Berg, That Berg . . .

Now, when the pack hits one of these bergs en masse, all-out if you're caught in the back, you lose about 3 minutes. So there is a huge slamfest before each one. Guys sacrifice their whole future to dive into every little hole to improve their position before a berg. So you see the most amazing acrobatics just before any of these hills—Good Lord, bikers and bikes flying all around, we're going about 80 kph, and I was sitting on the rainbow jersey's wheel. Rudy Dhaenens was looking down for a split-second and he hit a seam in the road. Boom! His hands came off the bars, his chest hits the stem so hard he just flips up into the air and lands face first on the highway. I saw this whole scene in that horrified, adrenal rush, slow-motion view you see through when you are about to eat it. His bike bounced then started sliding toward me. I inched past it and avoided the nastiness. About 40 guys who were on my wheel didn't avoid it and chowdered. Rudy looked like a rerun of Evel Knievel at Caesar's Palace when he missed the landing ramp. Can you put a price on suffering?

April 4

Left De Panne into a 100-kph head wind, no lie. The pack was creeping. That was fine with me. The problem is that after we do that Kemmel a couple of times, we have to come back to De Panne. So we do the Kemmelberg from two directions, and on the way back the pack explodes. I mean, you couldn't close a 3-inch gap to save your life. Phil and throbbing Sean Yates made the first group. The rest of our team was in the second group. We were chasing all right until it began to rain and sleet. The whole group dove into the hotel as soon as we got to the finishing circuit in De Panne. Soon after, so did Phil and Sean. Jelle Nijdam had the leader's jersey and won the stage hands down. Buckler and Panasonic rule these races, and today was no exception. Three Days of De Panne is so hard and nasty that to finish is a decent goal, to win is amazing. It is normally a preparation race for the Tour of Flanders, but every moment is like the Tour de France, except colder. Sunday is the Tour of Flanders, so since you have to be in the hotel on Saturday, you get one whole Friday to try and recover from this insanity. You get one day when you usually need about one *year* to recover from the Three Days of De Panne.

COBBLESTONE CLASSICS

April 5

Howlin' at the moon as a good Euro' dog should, all day doing laundry and gettin' ready for the Tour of Flanders this Sunday. I am so wasted that my head is ringing; then Noël calls up to inform me that immediately after Sunday's race, I have to drive to Paris and fly to Spain for the Tour of the Basque Country, a wicked, five-day stage race—then drive all night back to Paris for Paris-Roubaix next Sunday. Whoa now, I have been on morale-destroying death missions before, but this one might crack me for good. Seven years of pro biking haven't cracked me yet, so I guess I'll survive. The thieves of Zion who huddle at my door continually forget that Bobke is and always will be delivered by the prayers of the faithful.

April 6

Two hours easy training before going to the Holiday Inn, Ghent, this evening. I felt pretty good riding and did a few sprints for the legs to loosen up. Saw Greg L. in Ghent, by my crib, out shopping for his wife's birthday. He was in a full sweat from motor-pacing and he saw me first, so he comes screaming up yelling and scares the granola out of me. I say, "See ya on the cobbles, man!" He says, "For sure!" So I cruise down to the Holiday Inn, where about ten bike teams are staying for the race. What a zoo! Peter Post shows up at dinner and his Panasonic boys get deadly silent and serious. The stakes of this game are high and keep getting higher, and Post don't want no clowns screwing up the homicidal ambiance. As a matter of fact, whenever he looks at me, he just shakes his head in pure wonder. . . .

April 7

D-Day for all Euro' dogs: Tour of Flanders. Flanders is the world center for professional cycling, and the *Ronde van Vlaanderen* is *it*. Woke up, ate, then split Ghent for Saint Niklaas for the start. About 200,000 people jam in to the town square just to watch us sign in. When you sign in, you look out from the stage to this sea of people, and I always wave just to act like a rock star for a split second—nobody fathoming what the hell I'm doing. So we head out of town for 270 km of fun. The weather was cold, windy and rainy, which is as it should be. We hit the first feed zone flat out, and the pack was already coming to pieces. A few crashes that are inevitable didn't help keep things together, either. We had a long, flat cobble stretch before the first berg this year, and that broke the pack up some more. I took Phil to the front as often as I could, but the tempo was horribly fast and every man was for himself after the *Oude Kwaremont*—the traditional, first cobbled berg. Phil had to bridge up to the leaders by himself, and he was the last guy to make it. This year, the wind was really strong, and so there was no regrouping after the hills, as there most times is. I hung tough in my group and scaled all the early hills, which was edifying. Then Frankie Andreu and J.T. rode it in together. Edwig Van Hooydooy killed everyone. I mean he's in the final break with Rolf Gölz and Rolf Sorensen from Ariostea and Johan Museeuw from Lotto, and he just pedals away from them. Phil finished good in the first main pack, as usual. Another day on Flanders' Fields. I ain't even going to start in on that. . . .

April 10

I was excused from the Spain trip; but instead, there's Ghent-Wevelgem— 210 km in Flanders, Belgium. After two days in a coma, I wake up to find myself at this ancient velodrome, about 50 yards from the place where I stay up here. So I stroll over and sign up, no worries. Our game plan is the same as it has been all spring: Protect Phil for as long as possible. Ghent-Wevelgem this year has taken the Kemmelberg out of the race. I heard a lot of explanations, but never really understood, so we had a hard race, but not hideous. The only thing that split the pack was this *huge crash* that filled the whole road. Sean beefed it early on today and ripped a 12-inch by 4-inch patch of skin off his right shin. Ouch! Everyone except Phil got caught in the crash, and then Phil crashed in the finale. Today was not our day. Plus, the team that went to Spain has been decimated by a horrendous Euro-virus, and Brain is our only guy left in the race after only two days. This whole week is not our week.

April 12

Got up early to rendezvous with the cobbled classics crew in Kortrijk. We all got in the team cars and drove to Wallers, where the hardest cobbles begin during Paris-Roubaix. We rode the trial 100 km of Sunday's course. Geez, it was a dust bowl, even after just two or three guys passed in front of you. If you don't get any rain before Sunday, it will be hard to see your bars unless you're a lifer at Lille prison. We had fun torturing each other, as usual when we do these reconnaissance training rides. A few camera crews were about, as well as the Telekom, PDM and Panasonic teams. I felt pretty good for a change. On the last section of cobbles before Roubaix, I happened to see a bird carrying a twig for its spring nest. The twig was so huge that the little bird could hardly get off the ground. Message from your mama, bro'. . . .

April 13

Drove to Compiègne for the start of tomorrow's Paris-Roubaix. Rode for a couple of hours through this huge forest, but had to get back to town for the usual media circus team presentation. This practice has been banned before any other World Cup race, except for this one race, as usual. The French think that rules made to protect the riders don't apply to them.

April 14

Paris-Roubaix

- Geez, I felt bad today. After 100 km, I was already toasted. By the time we hit the first cobbles, I was already barely hanging on. Then I flatted at a very inopportune time and had to chase for about 20 km. I finally caught the peloton after the first feed zone, and promptly flatted again. I chased and chased and just caught the team cars at the entrance of Wallers Forest, and that was all she wrote for me today. Getting flats is part of this race—especially since it hasn't rained for so long the cobbles are sharp—and it is hard to avoid the potholes in the cloud of dust you ride in, unless you're at the very front. Today though, I felt so weak and worthless that I would have had to defy gravity just to finish. Steve motivated up there for fourth, and Sean was stomping—until he flatted and got run over by the blind skinhead from the Société du Tour de France, who was driving an official's car. Marc Madiot had no such trouble, and won his second Paris-Roubaix. That cobblestone trophy makes for quite a display on your kitchen shelf when the neighbors come over to gossip about the price of wine in China. . . .

INTO THE ARDENNES
April 16

Oh Lord, I am in trouble. I started feeling crappy last night, and at 7 p.m. went to bed feeling like I was about to puke. Then I got the chills. Then an acid, belly-like madness. I kept on sleeping on and off all night, awakening every few minutes by waves of fire in my belly. Because I have to travel to Liège today I decided to bag training and hope I feel better; but man, I don't know, I just don't know.

April 17

Flèche Wallonne

This race had two amazing elements. One was the weather: Sun, rain, hail, and in one corner, about 10 meters long, it snowed. Just on that one corner. The second amazing element was Moreno Argentin, who absolutely *slaugh-*

tered everyone. I didn't feel too bad after all, and did my usual teamwork for Phil without qualms. Phil was the only guy on our team to finish this race. As usual, at this time of year, the classics guys are tired and the stage race guys aren't on form yet. Any other implications are too frightening to consider.

April 18

Long, long Liège-Bastogne-Liège training ride today. We rode each and every hill of Sunday's race, in the pouring rain and wet snow. A total of 170 km, and I felt really good for the first time this year. My form is coming around, finally. So I just about sprinted up every hill, and just for grins tortured all the Z, Motorola, and Helvetia boys all day, because we all sort of intersected on the course. Had a good talk with Greg L. about fast cars, suicidal motorcycles, and strong bikers.

April 19

Did a very cold, 2-hour ride along the mighty Schelde canal through Gavere, Eke, Merelbeke, Ninove, Duerle, and back to Ghent. A total of about 1,000 people live in these towns, plus a few world champions, riders at the top of the world rankings, classic winners, and Tour stage dominators. Where I come from, I'm the only pro for about a million square miles. I felt pretty good and didn't get frostbite, so I am stoked to shred on Sunday.

April 20

Getting ready to go to Liège this morning, when Noël "Blowel" Dejonckheere calls and says I ain't going. Whoa, I've been kicked down and felt shitty before, but not quite this low. Oh well, I just did a small ride and took a 4-hour nap. Then at 10 p.m., Och' calls and says, "What the hell are you doing at home?" I go, "Noël told me I wasn't racing." Shit, our team is turning into Panasonic, or some shit!

April 21

Rode easy for an hour and watched L-B-L on TV. Argentin again slayed all. He is the King of the Ardennes without a doubt. Felt kind of like crap watching the race on TV, instead of being in there takin' names and ripping off legs.

April 23

Drove to the Netherlands to do Amstel Gold Race training on all the hills. I didn't feel too bad, but not really strong either. I was happy to be out there, until it started snowing on us. Here it is, almost May, and we're training in the snow still. This used to puzzle me, until I looked on a globe to find that the Netherlands is roughly the same latitude as Nome, Alaska. Then we drove to our hotel for tomorrow's race, the Scheldeprijs. What a devo den. This place makes the Roach Motel look like the Trump Towers.

April 24

270 km, Scheldeprijs, Antwerp, Belgium. Flaming fast start—whoa—we rode the first 100 km in 2 hours flat. My legs were aching, but I clung to the wheels. We did a couple of small hills, but they broke up the race due to the amazing tempo. I managed to stay in the front. We went easy through the feed zone, then ape hooey to the finish. I was happy to finish, and even got up there for the sprint won by Mario Cipollini, as usual lately. I am finally coming out of a long hibernation.

April 25

Met Yates at the Holiday Inn in Ghent, and went training in an icy, north-easterly wind that was ripping across Flanders. We rode out toward Eeklo to chill with Noel Foré's ghost. Coulda sworn I saw Eric De Vlaeminck oiling his chain in front of this huge mud bog. . . . *Mein vrouw* (wifey) made me and Sean some sandwiches and soup, then we went downtown on our bikes to check out Ghent for mellow shopping and hard-core spew. Saw lost tribe member Joe Parkin at English bookstore. Bought rough CD and smooth Belgian waffle, like a good Flemish dog. Even the sun was shining for a while, to make the day about as good as it gets in Flanders.

April 26

Drove to the Netherlands to slot into Amstel Gold Race hotel. Very, very nice converted farmhouse, with four-star restaurant and upper, upper crust clients draped here and there in obvious European poses. We suited up after lunch and went out riding for a couple of hours. I felt pretty good and put a lid on my spew. Dinner was a very formal affair, and I went psychologically underground in order to maintain the affected and stiff ambiance that we simple white trash crave, but never find. Most Dutch are cycling fanatics, and the chief chef here is no different. He came out of the kitchen to ask how our dinner was, and we all went bonkers—especially since our last hotel should have been condemned the day Fausto Coppi died. The wine was excellent, and, as usual, Dag ordered ketchup for his potatoes. The staff had never heard that particular request, and one by one came out of the kitchen to see the spectacle with their own eyes. Dessert was the only disappointment, being mixed fruit, while ten very decadent cakes were in plain view. Then we all went outside and fed money to these goats who were penned up in the backyard. We spent quite a bit of cash, but it was worth it.

April 27

Amstel Gold Race, in the Dutch province called Limburg. Last World Cup race of spring. Slept good last night and digesting food well in the morning. We all rode over to sign in—beneath a giant Amstel beer bottle—and waited for the race to start. We started pretty slow, which is a miracle for any classic. Soon enough, as we got near the hills, the speed picked up. I felt good, and had no problem staying near the front. We went across a road where some construction was going on, and the pavement was all torn up. For once, I didn't flat, but the pack broke up—due to the tempo and lots of guys flatting. On the next hill, M. Argentin, R. Alcalá, Stephen Hodge, Giorgio Furlan, et al broke away and got a minute's lead direct. Phil asked me to chase, and me, Andy Bishop, and Norm Alvis started flying. The break was hauling, but we closed some ground. On the next hill, me and Andy Bishop started flying. The break was seriously motoring, but we closed some ground. On the next hill, we blew, but not too bad. I started chasing again, and some Lotto guys and Norm came up, and we were going good. After 40 km all-out, we finally caught the break. Moreno wasn't too happy to see the whole peloton catch up. I laughed at myself for working so hard to catch Moreno's group, who just won both L-B-L and F.W. We still had 40 km to go, and I was pretty hammered, but I hung on for dear life to try and finish. Then, my tire luck ran out, and I flatted on the same unpaved section right before the hardest hill of the race. Fondriest, Maassen, Suykerbuyck, and Dirk De Wolf got away right there, as about 30 guys flatted. What a mess. Brian Holm waited at least 5 minutes for a wheel, because all the cars were stopped servicing flats. I waited and looked down the road, watching our mechanic run a half-mile in about 2 minutes, carrying a pair of wheels. That was pretty dang good, man! I got going and chased onto the back end of the field, and rode to the finish with the unlucky group. Phil, Steve, and Dag all finished up there, so our team did a good job, even though we didn't infiltrate the last break. I am totally stoked to slave all day, catch a very dangerous break and finish the race. I was momentarily delivered from my suffering today. I don't know how long my good legs will last, but I don't care. Today, at least, I was flying.

DICTIONARY OF BOBKE SPEAK

Abdo-something-or-other = Djamolidin Abdujaparov

Bobke = Flemish for Bobby

Brain = Brian Walton

Cipolla = (Onion in Italian) Mario Cipollini

Dag = Dag-Otto Lauritzen

Del Bongo = Del Tongo

Edwig Van Hooydooy = Edwig Van Hooydonck

Frankie = Frankie Andreu

GPM = Grand Prix de la Montagne (King of the Mountains)

Greg L. = Greg LeMond

J.T. = John Tomac

L-B-L = Liège-Bastogne-Liège

F.W. = Flèche Wallonne

Mau Mau Fondriest = Maurizio Fondriest

Nate = Nathan Dahlberg

Noël = Noël Dejonckheere

Norm = Norman Alvis

Och' = Jim Ochowicz

Phil = Phil Anderson

Rudy D. = Rudy Dhaenens

Scott = Scott McKinley

Sean = Sean Yates

Steve = Steve Bauer

Wookie = Ron Kiefel

CHAPTER 7

Bobke on the Defensive

In 1991, Bobke faced the harsh realities of European racing and found himself fighting hard to regain his place on the Motorola team.

August 2, 1991

Geez, the team must have screwed up somewhere, so I get to race again. The last pro race I did was June 15. So I'm jazzed to be down here in central Spain for the Tour of Burgos, with the lunkhead crew of out-of-work Motorola bikers. We are in the same devo den with Toshiba and Weinmann, which are both folding their teams. The soon-to-be-unemployed bikers, at this one marginal hotel, could fill a soup kitchen.

August 3

Stage 1

Stacked it, man, hard. Since it was 10 degrees hotter than hell, I went back to the car for about fifteen water bottles. As I was coming back through the follow cars to the group, the CLAS team director started yelling at me personally, so I looked over to see who it was, figuring I must have raced against him at some time. As I was trying to rack my seven-year-pro brain, I hit the only rock on 60 miles of brand new pavement and went flying head over heels—doing my best imitation of the Flying Wallendas, the day their Big Top burnt to the ground. Sheeeit!! I just lay there on the ground for about 10 minutes like a moron, shaking my head. As I lay there in the road with fresh slices of skin hanging off me, this little worm inched its way across the road under my legs. That little bastard was laughing at me, I swear to God. I squashed him flat and somehow felt better. Just as I caught the group, we started chasing like banshees so Stephan Joho could sneak away for the win, and I could dream about infected wounds and sawbone doctors.

August 4

Stage 2

A real mutha for ya today. We started way too fast, then a break got away without any of us. So before the three climbs in the finale, team director Noël Dejonckheere ordered a chase, presumably so our boy Andrew could win. So we chased for about 2 hours to bring things back together. Anyway, after the first two climbs, I was totally delirious, and on the descent leading to the final climb, I completely missed a turn. Luckily, Thomas Wegmüller was in my way, and I plowed into him and held on while he put me in the right direction. Unlucky for Thomas, because he beefed it. The last 17 km were straight up this mountain, and Gianni Bugno wasted all. The insane Spanish fans were too tanked to notice Pedro Delgado got dropped, and were deliriously screaming and pushing us up the hill. I suppose because of my Irish guilt complex, I refuse all pushes, but Roberto Pagnin, being Italian, has no such problem and came freewheeling past me on a 20-percent grade. I tried to tackle him, but it was all I could do just to pedal.

August 5

Damn it's hot, and the sun must be baking the boys' brains, because there were twenty crashes of varying degrees of seriousness. There is this one Spaniard who raced bikes against Moses and is still out here. His name is Angel Sarrapio, and he's about 80 percent blind. Whenever I am near him, I immediately try to get away from him. But I wasn't fast enough today and saw him disappear into a huge hole and come flying out, looking for road-rash revenge. It was funny, because he took out Sean Kelly and Federico Echave, both of whom he has slaved for in the past. Echave's bike slid right under my wheels. I was torquing on the bars so hard, my stem twisted over, but I was relieved to keep it up. Those guys came back to the group just as we wound up the finale—all covered in cuts, blood, diesel fuel, oil, and nasty Spanish dirt. Ouch. The finale featured some wicked huge pileups. With about 15 km to go, I barely avoided a massive pileup, but Per Pedersen didn't, and broke his lower leg, so the bones were sticking out. I thank God I didn't see this, but you could hear his screams from heaven to hell.

August 6

I was so wasted today, I just sat at the back and noodled in with the gruppetto. I hope I get used to this heat soon, or my brain is going to melt out of my ears. Since the boys did such a good job two days ago to chase the break, Andrew dropped out today. We are staying in the same hotel this whole stage race, or at least me and J.T. thought so. When we got back to our room after the stage, we heard what sounded like a river running through our room. Then, the Toshiba guys downstairs from us kept coming up to our room to look at our bathroom. We looked in their room on the way to dinner. It looked like Sea World without the dolphins! Lord have mercy, we laughed at that one. However, when we went upstairs after dinner, our room was totally demol-ished. And the sink, toilet, and bathtub were on top of our beds. So they moved us across town for a night. Or was that a nightmare?

August 7

Team time trial, 42 km

I felt much better today and cruised in the TTT. J.T. and Norm, especially, were pulling like fiends, and we did all right. Banesto went ape and creamed Gatorade, so Gianni Bugno had to give up his leader's jersey to Pedro Delgado. We rode back to our patched-up room, showered, ate, then went outside to get some air. While we were sitting there, some Mormon missionaries came up and introduced themselves. To see some all-American, Utah, Wonder Bread eating, Bible-thumping, Kmart-shopping kids in the middle of a European stage race in Spain . . . blew my mind. I mean, there is no escape, man.

August 8

Last stage, Tour of Burgos

The clouds rolled in and cooled things off, which was really nice. Plus the boys went really slow, until the last hill. I felt pretty good and did a big lead-out with Norm and Nate for J.T., for a hot-spot sprint. That was fun, especially since we didn't get dropped on the 10-km climb, 30 km from the finish. My form has improved each day here, so I'm stoked to do San Sebastian on Saturday.

August 10

San Sebastian World Cup

Woke up early, feeling pretty good. Saw homeboy No. 1, Rául. We are down like a tranqued rhino. Rode down to sign in with boys, who in 8 hours will be very tired men. I was stoked to see so many spectators from all over Europe. Miguel Indurain came over and said hello. I almost fell over, but played it cool and said, "Good job in the Tour de France," and all that good trash.

We started easy, but soon enough, guys were launching attacks and going for glory. I covered some moves according to the team plan, but none worked until Dick Dekker got away. The pack then settled down, and we went quite easy until the last 60 km . . . when we started flying. We did a few hard rolling hills, then went up the last hill faster than is humanly possible. I made it into the last gruppetto and we caught a big group . . . and me, Dag, Steve, and Nate all finished together. I am pleased to finish and actually surprised to have pretty decent form. We all sprinted back to the hotel to shower and got on the bus to fly to Lille. Another World Cup, and another million points for Gianni Bugno.

August 12

After one whole day of rest, I'm somewhere in the Netherlands for the prologue of the Tour of Holland. I went as hard as I could go and only lost 35 seconds in 4 kilometers to "Jelly Belly" Nijdam. These guys never cease to amaze me by how fast they can propel themselves on bicycles.

August 13

Stage 1

Mellow, almost easy, stage. We started fast, but it soon became evident that nothing would go up the road. There are generally two seasons in pro biking: before the Tour and after the Tour. This race is much easier than it would be if it were a few weeks earlier, because after the tour, the boys are generally annihilated physically, if not mentally as well. So the Tour of Holland is custom made for a born joker like me. We race hard, but the guys usually ride at a civilized pace.

August 14

Stage 2a

Forget what I said about us goofing around in this race, because we flamed start to finish today. Nate was the absolute hero of the day. After attacks were being launched from every guy in this field, Nate got away by himself. The pack sat up for a few kilometers, and Nate was flying. Then,

Bobke on the Defensive

Panasonic organized a big TTT, but they all blew chow before they caught Nate. We were stoked, because with 15 km to go, no teams were chasing and Nate had about 2 minutes. Then, out of the blue, Ariostea did a big chase and caught him with only about 4 kilometers to go. That's bikin', and Veenstra from Buckler won the stage.

Stage 2b

God, I was wasted in this time trial and went backwards, but made the time at least. Frans Maassen slayed all, and the great white hope Brain beefed it in the only corner in the 43 km TT.

August 15

Since I've been such a good pro, Och' just fired me today. I was bummed out and frowning heavily—for about five minutes. So I figured I'd attack and go out fighting at least. And that is just what I did. I went in about twenty breaks, and attacked solo a few times. One time, I got a pretty decent gap, but the race was pretty controlled and ended with a strange, ten-man break getting away in the finale. I got 12th in the field sprint—which was fun, but terrifying.

August 16

Damn fast, windy stage today. But I felt pretty good. I got in some excellent breakaways, but never with the right teams. With Tulip, Telekom, Buckler, Panasonic, PDM, TVM, Ariostea all going ape to be in the breaks, it is really hard and rare to be in the move that stays away. But I was stoked to get in a few breaks and not sit on the back the whole day. Theunisse made his big move today. I barely missed this traffic light, on an island in the middle of one blind corner, but Gerty went headfirst into it. He came back to the group bleeding from his head, like a stuck pig. Then he went straight to the front of the peloton, and the photographers descended like vultures to get this on film. They almost crashed him again, fighting for the best shot.

August 17

Last day, and I felt a bit sick—with a sore throat and all. I suppose this is a sign of better form, rather than fading form, since I've had exactly one good day since 1990. Anyway, I didn't want to push it and risk getting really sick, so after 150 km, I hit the showers. Maassen held on to win, and Eddy Schurer won the stage. I love the Tour of Holland, and I'm happy I got to do it one more time. I've been fired before, and yes, I'll be fired again.

August 20

Plouay

Flew to France somewhere, got dropped, showered, flew back to the Netherlands.

August 21

Veenendaal-Veenendaal 210 km, some hard hills and one nasty wind battle along these levee roads. I felt great today, and stayed in the front on all the hills. But after all that, the peloton stayed intact—until this weird, funky break of twenty guys noodled off the front on the flats, with 30 flat kilometers to the finish. Pro biking is just way too baffling. . . . Wiebren Veenstra got the flowers. I finished up, no worries. I wanted, at least, to finish my last race for a while. Flew home to Italy on the last flight from Zaventem to Milano, with a bunch of Italian shoppers. I was too melancholy to worry about crashing. Plus, there were three nuns and a priest on the flight, so no worries.

Bobke on the Defensive

October 13

Great balls afire!! The boys just couldn't live without me. The team called yesterday and said get on the plane for Paris-Tours. The peloton hasn't seen hide nor hair of Bobke for nine weeks. Every single biker went bonkers when they saw me. I was so stoked, man!! So we started pretty fast for a 290-km race. Then Chrisophe Lavainne got away and the tempo settled down. But Lavainne got up to a 28-minute lead. So the peloton started chasing, with about 130 km to go. I hung in there for dear life, until about 20 km to go. I blew so high, I could have been run over by flight #207-AF Paris–New York. But I ate some food and kept going. I caught four guys who had dropped on the last hills, and I finished. I was totally stoked to contribute and finish today, after so long without racing. Did four World Cup races this year now, and finished three, so I am cruisin'. So we all jumped in the team cars to blast back to Paris for our flights to Italy. We almost wrecked a few times, but made it to our flight about 30 seconds before it left. Sweeeeet. . . .

CHAPTER 8

Lost in the Jemez

It was a cold morning. Butt-ass cold, yet clear and not too windy, and that usually means a pretty decent afternoon in northern New Mexico, even in January. Anyway, that's what I told myself as I left home in Santa Fe for a long ride through the Jemez Mountains. With my route all planned out in my head, two water bottles, some food, and a five spot, I was set to jet. I left Santa Fe heading south on the frontage road that parallels I-25 toward Albuquerque. I felt okay, warming up on the rolling hills as commuters whizzed by, all rushing to work at 75 to 90 mph. In contrast, I pedaled leisurely along the freeway for about 30 miles, until I reached the Cochiti Lake turnoff. I turned right and headed due west toward Cochiti Dam. There was a slight head wind, but as I crested the climb to the dam, I began to feel good.

When I say good, I mean I began to fly. The entire previous year had been a struggle. I felt bad in just about every race. Even at the California training camp I had just returned from, I felt bad . . . tired . . . lethargic. But today, my form returned—big time. I was pushing a huge gear into the wind and no matter how hard I pushed, my legs begged for more. *That* is form. For an entire year, all my bros on the circuit were asking me, "How's the form?" And for a year, all I could do was bow my head and say, "Shitty." But not today. Today I had wings. And on these wings, I flew headlong into the Jemez.

I came to the town of Cochiti and had to force myself to stop at the 7-Eleven. I wanted to keep blasting, but I knew this was probably the last outpost of supplies for many miles, and I wanted to ask the locals about the road conditions ahead. They had no idea what I was talking about. The store clerks just shook their heads and looked at me in this strange way. I figured either I was making a big mistake by proceeding, or fifth-generation Spanish conquistadors didn't make it a priority to communicate with a Lycra-clad, possibly insane, bike geek. My logical mind, high on good form and therefore only marginally functioning, opted for the latter explanation. . . .

So I kept biking, past Cochiti Lake, past the dam, over the Rio Grande, and into the foothills of the mountains. I still felt good and was making great time, when I came upon a work crew that was repairing the road. I thought I might stop and get a second opinion, but as I approached they all stopped their work to stare at me. I decided it would be totally cool just to fly by without saying a word to create a ghostly impression. I figured I succeeded, as they all signed the cross when I passed.

As the pavement gave way to a dirt road, I climbed a long ridge and then dropped into a pretty little orchard filled with trees and a few rancheros. I came around a blind turn where a red-tailed hawk was chewing on a rodent. The hawk flew up in fright, almost taking my head off. Whoa. I could have counted his talons if I hadn't been busy shitting myself. The valley was only a few miles long, and I came to a little ranchero at the far end. The rancher had erected a sign that read, "Do not proceed without proper four-wheel-drive vehicle. If you break down, do *not* ask for assistance here. *You have been warned.*" I figured the rancher was either totally antisocial or I was in deep shit. Still feeling strong, I opted for the former.

I did pause, though, considering the situation . . . but these kinds of days of great form are rare and I didn't want to break my rhythm by turning around—not just yet, anyway. So I continued throbbing straight into the Jemez, sacred mountains to the Tewa tribes and nuclear scientists.

As the orchard valley gave way to the mountains, I began a long climb on the dirt road. The air became crisp, and snow began to line the roadside, and it soon changed to hardpack snow. After 10 miles or so, a foot of fresh powder covered the hardpack. There were two tire grooves visible down the middle of the now snow-covered road. As long as I kept my bike in one of the tire grooves, I continued to make good time. This went on for many miles, until I came to a Forest Service gate closed across the road. Beyond the gate was an ocean of pristine powder snow. I decided to proceed. By doing so, I learned that looking at a map in your living room while watching reruns of "The Three Stooges" is a hell of a lot different than actually following the route.

I had plotted out a course from Cochiti northwest through the Jemez Mountains that eventually crossed Highway 4 and came out of the mountains just west of Los Alamos. Then I'd ride to San Ildefonso Pueblo to meet my friends and eat dinner before getting a ride home to Santa Fe. Since I had been blasting hard, making great time all morning, and was high up in the mountains, I figured that the highway and Los Alamos couldn't be far away. I looked at my watch and it read 12:30 p.m. I had been going hard for 5 hours. Little did I know I had 12 to go. . . .

I jumped over the gate, hoisted my bike on my shoulder and began to hike. The hike wasn't too bad to begin with. I was still able to follow the road as I post-holed up to my knees, and I could make out the outline of the road snaking through the trees. I hiked for hours, making slow but steady progress and leaving the only set of tracks since last November. Nothing had passed through here for at least three months. I had my head down, carrying my bike and trudging through the snow, when I was over-come by sudden fear. I stopped, looked around, and found myself in the middle of a ghost town. Whew.

After I caught my breath and looked around, I thought it was pretty cool—but I hurried through anyway. By now, the sun had noticeably begun to set. Also, up until now the road twisted and turned through the mountains, and I decided a more direct, due north route would get me to Los Alamos quicker. So I left the road and pointed myself in what I thought was the most direct path north. I had made a number of bad decisions, but this was by far the worst. The hike now became very difficult, with steep climbs and rugged descents. The climbs were manageable, but as my cycling shoes became frozen solid and caked with ice, the descents were nearly impossible to negotiate and I tumbled countless times. I still felt pretty strong, but this constant falling took the edge off my resolve.

After climbing another of the neverending ridges, I thought for sure the paved highway couldn't be far. So I climbed a tree to look out. My heart sank as I gazed upon endless trees, ridges, and snow. Not one building, not a single lightpost or telephone pole. The sun was really sinking now and giving off its last rays of light for the day. My steps took on a desperate tempo as nagging little voices of doom began to invade my logical mind.

By now, my wife was freaking. I was already a couple of hours late to San Ildefonso—and my friends there knew the Jemez Mountains well. I was also beginning to get nervous. The sun dipped behind the horizon, creating a beautiful *alpenglow,* and it reminded me of the very real possi-bility of spending a night in the snow-covered mountains with only my Lycra clothing and plastic helmet. I knew this might push my wife into the drowning pool of mental dysfunction, so I kept going.

The nagging voices had now turned into siren blasts of fear. I climbed another steep ridge and, catching the very last rays of light, looked out into the same endless mountains. I climbed a tree just in case I might see something, *anything,* and reflecting on my situation realized I was *totally* lost and needed help. When the top of the tree I was perched in snapped off and I was pitched to the ground, I knew I had gone too far to turn back. . . .

San Ildefonso is one of the Indian pueblos in northern New Mexico along the Rio Grande. It was also my destination when I set out that morning. Chiara, my wife, had already telephoned our friends there about 100 times to see if I had arrived. She was frantic, having no way of knowing what might have happened to me. Was I run over somewhere, lying in a ditch? Was I dehydrated and hypothermic somewhere in the mountains? Had I crashed and broken something? She was lighting votive candles and praying to every saint she knew. At the the the same time, there were some serious discussions going on back at San Ildefonso as to where the heck was that crazy bicycle racer. . . .

After hitting the ground, I checked to see if I had broken anything falling out of the tree. Luckily, the pine boughs had slowed me down enough to prevent any broken bones. I just sat there in despair, holding my head in my hands. I couldn't comprehend how a day that started out so well could turn so bad. These thoughts soon exploded into a synopsis of my cycling career and my life in general. I had hit just about rock bottom. Then I heard the first sound since the hawk screeched, which seemed like a decade ago. It was a crow.

The crow was flying straight south. I saw him look at me, make a sharp turn, swoop down, do a 360-degree circle around my head, and fly off due north. I ignored this, not knowing for certain if it were real or just my imagination; but when he did the exact same maneuver again, I took it as a sign, a sort of flying road map. The crow's direction after he circled my head was actually quite different than the one I was taking. But I put my logical faith in the thought that crows have to eat and garbage dumps are much easier pickings than a frozen forest. I put my spiritual faith in the thought that the local Indians had been here one hell of a lot longer than I had.

So, with better morale, I began hiking again. I continued to struggle up the hills and stumble down the descents. After hours of this in complete darkness, I began to see the folly in following the crow. I sat down and felt some real deep bone fatigue. I looked down in despair and saw deer tracks in the snow leading up a steep draw. I decided to follow those since the going would be much easier if I didn't have to post-hole each step. I looked at my watch. It read almost 10 p.m. Fourteen hours so far. I decided not to look again.

Because the deer tracks were headed in the same general direction as I was and because they made the going much easier, I regained some of my lost resolve. The draw was long and steep, but at the top I could make out a road cut through the

☆　☆　☆

I was grasping at possible explanations and came up with one: I died and St. Peter had come to get me in a four-wheel-drive Bronco. I finally decided that, no, St. Peter would at least be driving a Rolls Royce.

trees—the road I had so stupidly abandoned many hours ago. I was so jacked up I bounded along, my bike suddenly weightless, no longer feeling hungry or tired. When I found tire tracks coming from the north, I knew I had made it. I could even ride my bike again and was plowing along as happy as I've ever been on a bicycle. I flashed back and felt the joy of the first moment I learned to ride solo.

Then I saw them. A pair of headlights coming toward me. This took me by surprise to say the least. I was a little freaked out and got off the road to let them pass. They slowed and came to a stop with the headlights shining in my face. I saw a driver and a passenger looking at what they might be considering wasn't actually there. We stared at each other for a few moments, until the passenger rolled her window down and said, "Aren't you Bob Roll?" My mind went haywire trying to comprehend the situation. I was grasping at possible explanations and came up with one: I died and St. Peter had come to get me in a four-wheel-drive Bronco. I finally decided that, no, St. Peter would at least be driving a Rolls Royce. So I said, "Why, yes, I am." Then they said to hop in the wagon and we'd go to their house to warm up and they'd give me a ride to Los Alamos. I sort of paused, slack-jawed, and looked over my shoulder to see if Rod Serling was nearby, playing his "Twilight Zone" music. I threw my bike in the back and jumped in, transformed instantly from possible coyote meat to a celebrated bike racer.

It turned out that Gary and Lynn Clark were bike riders from California, recently transferred to Los Alamos, and had been following my race career for some time. They had a rustic cabin, without a phone, about 20 miles out of Los Alamos, where I changed into some warmer clothes. I wanted to call Chiara to tell her I wasn't at the bottom of some coyote's belly or a mangled mess in some desolate roadside ditch—or whatever her imagination had conjured up by now. I'm sure I was a ranting lunatic as the Clarks drove me back to Los Alamos. We stopped at a phone and I called Mark Swazo to drive up from San Ildefonso and take me home to Santa Fe. I'm sure I was still ranting all the way back to Santa Fe.

I got home about 1 a.m.—nearly 17 hours after I left. I had some gnarly frostbite on my ankles, as they had been packed in snow for the whole time in the mountains, but otherwise I wasn't too badly off. It took a long time for me to calm down and go to sleep, even though I was physically exhausted. Just before I dozed off, I realized people will continue to do foolish things like I did . . . but it really helps to have friends in spiritual places.

CHAPTER 9

Bobke Takes to the Dirt

Homey Sean Yates called up today from Scottsdale, Arizona. He's visiting a Motorola factory, getting covered in germs, shaking hands and signing photos, for green card borderline bootleggers who never heard of Paris-Nice, the Scheldeprijs, or the Tour of Flanders. Anyway, he was just checking in on the peloton's wayward son. He asks, "What are you doing this year?" Then I dropped the bomb on him—"I'm racing for Greg LeMond on the dirt and Team Z in some road races." I said, "I'll see you out in Cali' tomorrow." He was *dipped in shit!*

Nice and mellow early flight to Frisco. I checked into my suite overlooking Santa Rosa, then suited up to go biking with Greg and Johan Lammerts. We rode like mad men for 5 hours over all these mountains around here. I felt decent and didn't get dropped, even though I wanted to. From my hotel room window, I can look down the hill to the parking lot of the hotel below us where the Motorola crew gathers each morning for their training ride. So when they were all gathered, I began bellowing directions of where and how to stick it. They knew the voice, but couldn't see the face. They recognized the dialect, but refused to believe their ears. Bobke just won't die. . . .

Due to a publicity photo shoot this afternoon, we planned a 3-hour ride up the Geysers and back. On the way out, we intersected with half of the red-white-and-blew crew. So S. Bauer started flaming up the Geysers and dropped all his teammates—except Brian Walton, Johan L. and, the envelope please, Bobke . . . sweet. Did some off-road photos with Graham Watson, which was pretty painless until I fell out of this freaking, moss-covered tree while I was clowning around.

★ ★ ★

I mostly prayed not to get dropped—is that a sin?

January 19

Last night, the Z team director Roger Legeay showed up with soigneur Otto Jácome; and Greg and Johan got silent and serious. So today we did a 6-hour ride in 4.5 hours. Ouch. I was wasted when we got back to the hotel. So I ate about 14,000 calories just to make sure I don't get deficient in any vitamin category. You never know, eh? Roger and Otto left this afternoon so we went out for Mexican fast food and a movie. We almost missed the movie 'cause Greg got waylaid by autograph pilgrims.

January 20

Took a day off and went to mass with my sister, brother-in-law, and great aunt—who all live in Santa Rosa. I mostly prayed not to get dropped—is that a sin?

January 21

Smokin' 7-hour ride. As usual, we raced up all the hills, but today as an added bonus we raced on the flats, as well. We rode out to the coast on these narrow, hilly roads, then back along this *really* narrow, *really* hilly road. I felt lame for the first 5 hours, then started to put a boot in it back to Santa Rosa. When we got back, Sean Y. called, and I said come up to chow. So we all started drinking and eating and telling boring stories of sin and redemption. Then our busboy from El Salvador has an epileptic fit in the kitchen and we all run back there to help. I was leaning over him when he came out of it and he goes, "Oh Lord, I guess I didn't make it to heaven."

January 22

Did 3 hours of mountain biking on private land, with some locals, around Occidental. The sun was shining and we all had a great time chasing overly nervous sheep. I guess some bikers have come through here before. Anyway, the ocean views were great—only obstructed by a few poison dog carcasses hanging from barbed wire.

January 25

Last day of camp and I was feeling pretty good pedaling back to the hotel—until one of the local pinheads in a pickup took exception to my existence on the same stretch of road and hooked me into the curb. A few stitches later, I am getting the hell out of California. Flew back to Santa Fe, New Mexico, and got all my gear in a van, and me and my frau moved to Durango, Colorado. I hope the Four Corners drivers enjoy my Celtic-German looks, chipped-tooth smile, and Northern Italian arm gestures more than the ones in Santa Fe.

January 31

Flying to "Sweet Home" Alabama on an MD88, one sweet airplane. I've never been to the Deep South, but I've heard a lot about it. Anyway, I'm doing a clinic and having a good ol' time yammerin' . . . with Erskin Caldwell's progeny. I ate some grits, drank some Budweiser, and had a great time where they love the governor . . . ooh, ooh, ooh.

February 14

Long, long, long drive to Van Horn, Texas. What a place! I got my bike out and went for a little ride through this dusty freeway stopover. I spotted a run-down little bar called El Gallo. I was going to go in to shoot some pool, but I looked in the window at a pile of Pancho Villa's grandchildren and decided a Lycra-clad bike wanker would probably not get to play too much pool before he got his ass whipped, so I just went to the hotel and tried to sleep; interrupted only a few times by dreams of careening big-rigs leveling roadside, shantytown hotels.

February 15

My mountain bike debut at Lajitas, Texas. This was a circuit race that was not too technical and had only a bit of singletrack. The boys started fast and I tried to stay near the front. Directly, there were only six of us left in the front. Then, on the last lap, only me and Rishi Grewal and Lance Armstrong were left in front. I had a flat, but I tried not to show it . . . until I washed out through some corners. So I had to let Lance and Rishi go. Then, on the last corner, I had to let three others go by. At the finish, I had to let go with a string of expletives. . . .

February 16

This 35-mile cross-country race was a blast. We actually started pretty mellow, then Dave Wiens went ape and after about 30 seconds there were five of us left in front. Wiens kept tanking, and he and Rishi got away from John Weissenrieder, Lance, and me. Then Lance flatted, and then John flatted. Then I saw Wiens up the road and caught him, and we cruised for a while, trying to catch Rishi. The last 10 miles of the course were the same for all categories, and I almost plowed into about twenty of the sport riders—but I kept the knobby side down and finished second. I showered and hit the road 15 minutes later—Euro-pro style. The folks we met were really nice and I can feel the iron death grip of paranoid Euro' psychosis loosening itself from my cranium.

March 13

Time trial stage, Cactus Cup

I ain't superstitious, but a black cloud just crossed my path. I woke up this morning a little tired from the long drive down here to Scottsdale, Arizona. But I rode out to the time-trial course to warm up, then did a couple of laps with John Tomac on the 5-mile course. I planned on taking this race pretty easy to get a feel for the dirt and avoid the cactus. I avoided the cactus all right, but after about 3 miles of the TT, I saw my one-minute man Jan Wiejak, and then Don Myrah—who started 2 minutes before me. I thought they were either going slow . . . or I was going pretty well. Anyway, I got all jacked up and hit a little whoop-de-do way too fast and washed out the front end, landing on my elbow. I jumped up, and when I reached down to put my chain back on, this stream of blood came shooting out of my arm like a crimson water fountain. It didn't hurt, so I kept pedaling. As I pedaled to the finish, I tried to hold the cuts, but when I finished, I was covered in blood. I went over the first-aid tent, and sat down. Each time my heart beat, blood was shooting across the parking lot, so I lay down. I guess it looked pretty bad, and everyone turned sorta pale when they saw me. The ambulance came and got me. We went to some hospital and I got stitched up—no worries. I went back to the hotel and my frau went out and got me some soup and tortellini at Guido's Deli. At least I didn't lose my appetite. . . .

March 14

Had a rough night of horrible dreams: watering green lawns in the desert with my blood and being run down by huge Cadillacs covered with blue hair. I've got to get out of Scottsdale, but I had to lay low today and be content with flashbacks all day. All my homies came by to check in on me, which was sweet. Man, I've crashed all over the planet. I've crashed into cars, boats, fences, trees, spectators, teammates, coaches, ditches, cats—and nothing ever happened. I've been racing mountain bikes for four weeks and so far I've got 18 stitches, a cracked elbow, severed arteries . . . and lost a busload of skin. I've got to suck it up, man, this is one hard sport.

☆ ☆ ☆   ☆ ☆ ☆

CHAPTER 10

Deep Down Dirty
with Bobke

Extracts from Bob Roll's diary in his first season on the Grundig World Cup circuit.

SPRING IN EUROPE

April 20, 1992

Got in the vomit comet to fly from Durango to Denver. A storm was brewing, so that eight-seat bug swatter was pitching all over the sky, for 1 hour and 23 minutes. Sheeeeiittt! I didn't like it, but I played it cool, while all the greenhorns puked up the red chili they just ate during their Southwest stay. I love the smell of bile in the morning . . . it smells like . . . tourism. Flew on to Chicago on some massive hurling stone, pretty smooth though. Then got on this huge Boeing aircraft to fly to Zaventem (the airport at Brussels, Belgium), over the Atlantic, with a pile of EuroTrash. Since the Gulf War and the dollar took a dive, these flights are full of Eurodogs and very few Americans . . . and only one long-legged, Resistol-snortin', Panhandle Slims and denim-clad Tour de France vet.

April 21

Landed in Belgium. It was raining, Sheeit!!! Got on the train to Kortrijk and slotted into Greg L.'s plush crib. I wanted to go for a ride, blast the stereo, watch some videos and eat at Q-Burger . . . but all I could do was a face-plant in the bed and sleep for 20 hours straight. I tried to sleep on the plane, but no dice—not even with the help of four Halcyons. Hope I didn't sleepwalk and Uzi the neighbors.

☆   ☆   ☆

Blasted down the E40 at 220 kph to my Mountain Bike World Cup debut. Get out of my way all you Fiat-drivin', beer-swillin', assembly-line cretins!

April 24

Blew up Greg's van on the way to Houffalize, so I had to rent a car at the airport. I strolled over to Hertz and said, "I want a large American car for three days." They said, we don't have any American cars, only Ford Scorpios. I looked at these Belgian rental car clerks and said, "That would be fine; give my condolences to Henry Ford." Blasted down the E40 at 220 kph to my Mountain Bike World Cup debut. Get out of my way all you Fiat-drivin', beer-swillin', assembly-line cretins!

April 25

If you did not finish in the top 50 of last year's Grundig World Cup series, you have to do a qualifier today for tomorrow's World Cup race. There were three heats of about 150 guys each, and they took the 80 fastest guys out of all three heats. Just what you want to do before a World Cup mountain bike race is to battle with 150 psychos for 35 places in your heat, man. So I lined up in the back of my heat and tried to pass as many guys as I could in 2 hours of racing. All my road buddies were in my heat, so I saw some of those philistines: Stefano Giuliani, Gilles Sanders, Ludwig Wijnants, Claudio Vandelli, Ennio Vanotti. Usually, I would spend about three-quarters of the race talking to them, but today I spent exactly zero seconds talking to *anyone*. It was balls to the walls direct from the start, and I tried to pass as many guys as I could and wound up around 30th to get a spot in tomorrow's race. *All right!*

April 26

Grundig World Cup No. I, Houffalize, Belgium

Woke up in the attic of this totally cool, 900 A.D. castle—often dreaming of being flogged by monks with brown-hooded robes and Roger De Vlaeminck's forehead—and went down to breakfast with the Tomes and Mrs. Tomes. I haven't been this nervous since my first communion, but tried to play it cool anyway. The race started fast as usual, straight up a road I once descended in Liège-Bastogne-Liège, and I was already barely hanging on after the first quarter-mile. The first lap, I was moving up steadily, even though I was suffering like a pig. I went steady the second lap, but had to ease way off on the third—'cause I felt a bonk coming on. I felt better on the last lap, and moved up to 33rd. That was okay, but at least I don't have to do another qualifier on Wednesday for the Dutch World Cup in Landgraff, a few days from now. Johnny T. wasted all—as only he can.

April 30

Grundig W.C. Landgraff, the Netherlands

The sun came out this morning, but the course was still pretty wet from three days of rain. The start was on this weird combo horseracing track and drive-in movie theatre—where's Joe Bob Briggs? Another wicked mondo start, and I got off the line pretty well. I hung in there all right and finished 18th . . . not too bad. I didn't beef it once, and passed a pile of bonk and crash victims. These starts are killing me. I usually need about 200 km to warm up, but here you get about 200 millimeters. If I don't get used to sprinting all out from the giddyup, it will be a long, cruel summer.

Bobke II

May 6

Woke up early for train ride from Greg's pad in Kortrijk to Switzerland. Since my bike is all packed up and I don't know the bus schedule, I had to hitchhike to the train station. Some old geezer smokin' a roll-your-own stogie stopped and piled me and all my gear into his 1965 Citroen low rider. He was spewing about the 1939 Tour de France, and since it was already 8:30 a.m. he was *tanked,* man. Had a nice long, mellow train ride to Zürich. Checked into this pension hotel for junkies and tried to sleep, while starving hop-head artists drowned in their own fluids. Slept for about half an hour, with my wallet tied to my clut sac.

May 10

Grundig World Cup, Klosters, Switzerland

Nervous as a balloon in a pin factory. Anyway, the boys started *mondo* as usual, and I avoided a gnarly fifty-man pileup in the first 100 yards. I was going well in 10th after one lap, but flatted at the beginning of the second lap. I never used a CO_2 gizmo before and guys were streaming past me as I sat there trying to fix it. The freaking cartridge froze to my fingers and peeled five layers of skin while I shook it loose . . . sweet. I got going again and started sprinting way too soon, I guess, and with a lap to go, I got a *fringale* to wake the dead (that is, a bonk so wicked your nerve endings are screaming so loud all the dead wake up and say, "Whoa, put that poor bastard out of his misery."). Anyway, I started crashing and hitting trees and spectators. I missed one drop-off and blew into the crowd and landed on this little kid. His giant Swiss dad got pissed at me when the kid started to cry. I said, "Hey man, go watch a chess game, you massive, Swiss butt-cheese." I pedaled on to the finish with Swiss track star Urs Freuler, who got the most cheers of anyone—except maybe J.T., who killed everyone once again. This was the nicest race yet, and for once in my life, the Swiss weather was super fine.

EAST COAST

June 6

There is this toxic, yellow clay back East, here in the Catskill Mountains, and today we got to plod through it for 4 long, gnarly hours. Back East, there are also the slime-covered, crumbling, shale waterfalls that we got to tumble down and curse the hippie pinheads who designed this disaster area. Also back East, there are these peaceful, tree-lined trails and babbling brooks that we might have gotten to ride—except for the Noahesque rain that turned them into rivers and rock- and root-strewn mud bogs that not even an agile pig should be herded through. I felt okay until the first dismount and mile run. I went from 5th to 50th, and I was cursing, bros. I kept cursing, but got a decent rhythm going and finished 18th, anyway. The race was about half running, and it has been a long time since I ran for 2 hours in a day—and I hope it is a long time before I do it again . . . a long time. The winner's average speed was 8.3 mph. Give me a break. No, give me a baseball bat so I can hammer somebody's legs for a while. Right now, I'm 26th on the planet in mountain bike racing and 6th overall on NORBA points—I'll be dipped in the bottom of Noah's Ark.

☆   ☆   ☆

> **There are also the slime-covered, crumbling, shale waterfalls that we got to tumble down and curse the hippie pinheads who designed this disaster area.**

June 7

Got out of a car last night, after driving from Hunter, New York, to Philly, so full of mud my stomach was the size of the Fuji blimp. I felt so bad I had to have eight double shots of tequila to dilute it and stay up to 3 a.m. listening to soul music on some radio station sponsored by Schlitz Malt Liquor, so I could be ready for CoreStates today.

All night, I sat in my bed listening to this smokin' rockin' blues station, while my head did laps around the hotel. I decided to call them and make a request. I had to let it ring for about 45 minutes, through this long set of working-class blues. Finally, this woman deejay with rhythmic, molasses-and-syrup-on-a-slow-boil-in-a-silver-spoon voice comes on the line—all sugary, but not one bit sweet, and says, "Congratulations. You've just won tonight's contest for tickets to this weekend's concert. Who's this" I say, "Bobke." "Where are you from Bobke?" I say, "Durango." She goes, "Huh?" I say, "Durango, Colorado . . . Four Corners, USA." She thought that one over for a while. Batting her smoke-dripping eyelashes and licking her heroin-twisted chops, she goes, "What are you doing here?" I told her about Hunter Mountain and the pro champs and all that good trash, and she said, "Well, I guess you can go to the show." I said, "I don't give a flying bag of crap about your disco-rock-concert-dance-club-laser-show contest. All I want is to hear 'Blue Moon,' by Billie Holiday." Click. Woke up 3 hours later, ate one egg, two pieces of toast with butter and strawberry jelly, and eight cups of coffee with 100 road guys that looked so tidy I thought I'd stumbled into a Young Republicans convention. Then I pumped up my skinny tires and split to the start. All I could do was sit on the curb with 1,500 homeless people, under the Liberty Bell. Let freedom ring. . . .

They said, "Go," and I almost got dropped in the first mile. I was dead last, but barely hanging on, ready to puke my guts out. I hung on, and after five or six laps I began to feel better. I kept feeling better throughout the race, and the last time up the Wall I was flying. At the top of the last passage, I was in the front group of about 15—and one of the only Americans. I couldn't believe it. Some small groups caught us and Bart Bowen launched solo . . . and Coors Light, Motorola, Spago, and the Sheriffs didn't chase—which I didn't believe, either. I wasn't about to chase, since my nearest teammate was in Normandy, France. My group sprinted it in, and Phil "the Dill" Anderson got us. Not a bad race, and for a while on the last lap, I was about to embarrass a whole lot of Young Republicans. . . .

June 20

Grundig W.C. Mont-Ste.-Anne, Canada

Been up here in Canada for a week or so, enjoying the Quebecoise hospitality. Just finished a stage race around Lake Placid, put on by a bunch of douche bags. Suffice it to say I will never do the Tour of the Adirondacks again—ever. Been eating fancy, French cuisine at this real posh restaurant near the hotel, scaring the bisque out of the local bourgeoisie. I'm like their worst nightmare—a cracker with a credit card. Anyway, the course was laid out very nice and I've been stoked all week about the race. So today we started with a mad dash up this nearly vertical climb that leveled off into a mud bog—bonus. I was cruising along pretty well—interrupted occasionally by the lapped females, some of whom required stiff-arming into the bushes, except Lisa Muhich, who is one of my stone homies and would stiff-arm me off a ravine if I ever tried anything like that. I kept blastin' away and moved up toward the top 10, until I broke my chain at the start of the last lap. *Porca miseria!* I almost had an aneurysm. I've raced bikes all over the planet and never broken a chain—ever. I left my chain at the bottom of some mud puddle and coasted down to the hotel. I was dipped in chain lube!

I was more than a little bummed, so I went to this bar to sip some ancient cactus juice and chill with my boyzzz. . . . Then this *flying hi, whaling, smoking* band called the Paul Deslauriers Blues Band began to shred. I did some crowd surfing—and had a great time with all the bikers, including Thomas "Frishy" Frischknecht, who creamed the field today.

That band had not been exposed to madly thrashing bikers and were about to walk off . . . until I decked the bouncer and kindly asked them to continue. They obliged.

June 27

Grundig W.C. Mount Snow, Vermont

Been spending the week with Johnny T. and his crew, Dave "Pope" Richards and Bike Bob Gregorio, at their condo here in Mount Snow. Hanging with the Tomes is so sweet, because I have no idea what is going on and he doesn't say jack. We did some good training rides and some acid-rain fishing. Then, we all went to play some pool and drink some Rolling Rocks, but I couldn't enjoy it that much—due to the fact that the clouds that blew in began to piss down. For a moment, I dreamt I was a camel driver in the desert, and was delivered from the heat by the purifying rain. But only for a moment.

This morning, I did a good warm-up and went to race. We started like bezoomy madness, straight up this wall and then down through the trees. I felt all right and started well and didn't lose too many places on the descent. Frishy roached his stem or something and came flying past on the second hill. I was going pretty well, but got a little too jacked up and went over the bars in the woods on the second-lap descent, looking like a spastic acrobat from the Irish-German, Oakland-Durango circus. Spectators were thick as mosquitoes on the descent, especially near the more dangerous sections, as usual. I landed on this thin tree that had been sawed off two inches above the ground, and tore a massive chunk of flesh off my skinny white ass. Luckily, about 2 minutes later, I went over the bars again . . . and filled my bleeding cuts with fine Vermont mud. Unluckily, I knocked the wind out of myself and could barely pedal up the next climb, and got passed by about twenty guys.

Deep Down Dirty with Bobke

J.T. was flying and basically peppering the field, as if he were giving a lesson to naughty children—until a possessed paparazzo figured his photo opportunity would be best served on the other side of the fastest downhill singletrack, and ran across the trail. J.T. was in full scoop mode and *whaling* down the descent and he *creamed* into the dude, tacoed his front wheel, sheared off his front brake, and came as close to cursing as he ever has.

I kept hanging in there and finally felt better on the last lap, and passed a pile of guys to get a decent placing. Then I showered up ASAP, got in my friend's—the Pepe's—car, and split for Albany, New York, to fly home. Tomorrow morning, I'll be at the "Durango Diner" eating bacon, eggs, and hash browns smothered in green chili; drinkin' coffee; snortin' gin; playing pool; and cowboy dancing with my sweet frau in the awesome Southwest. So all you insomniac air traffic controllers, jaded stews, drunken pilots, and muscle-bound, brain-dead baggage handlers, *get out of my way!* I'm going to *sweet home Durango!*

CHAPTER 11

Living in a Lactic-acid Crippling Haze

Bob Roll concludes extracts from his 1992 diary.

July 10, 1992

In February, when we moved to Durango, the relatively quiet spring road rides did not prepare me well for the summertime mayhem of Winnebago hell I experienced today, while driving to Crested Butte for the Fat Tire Festival. The mountain passes that I and J.T. had pedaled up in snowy splendor last winter were clogged with huge houses on wheels, driven by photo-opportunistic, camcorder-totin' lunkheads, who made a 4-hour drive take 7 hours. Anyway, I got to Crested Butte, slotted into the crib, and went to sign in and look at tomorrow's time-trial course—except nobody knew where the course was, so I cruised the beautiful and very rugged trails around town . . . *very* rugged.

July 11

Today, we did the first two stages of the Fat Tire Festival. The weather was dry for a change and the crit was fast. We blasted out of town like we just robbed the local Conoco gas station, up this little hill, down a pond road, and over this 2-inch-wide, fast bridge, and into single file—it was hectic. I started okay, and avoided a few wrecks, and was in a group of five guys,

Living in a Lactic-acid Crippling Haze

6th through 10th place. I thought, all right, I'm going good and I'll shred the last two laps. Then it happens . . . ppphhhiffffff. Sheeet, a freakin' *flat,* man! You can't just put your finger up and have some foaming-at-the-mouth mechanic run up and change your wheel so I got out my CO_2 cartridge and tube, lost about 5 minutes, and cursed through my grinding teeth for the umpteenth time this season. Cruised back to the hotel and sat there feeling like an idiot. Ned flatted, too, so I didn't feel quite so bad.

Time trial: This course was sooo sweet. A wicked, 10-inch-wide, 3-mile goat path, through aspens and *high* weeds. I felt tired, and cruised through it, only crashing into a few trees. Rishi blasted it to hand Ned a rare, high-altitude loss. I rode so poorly in the technical sections, I was bummed. Sometimes I ace the tricky stuff, but not today. . . .

July 12

Cross-country: Have *mercy!* What a race! Early start, and I guess the promoters forgot that no restaurants in this town open before 8 a.m. on Sundays during the summer—which made it difficult to digest pancakes, eggs, bacon, toast, and hashbrowns before 9 a.m. We started fast, as usual, and I was choking down bile after 100 yards, as the Greybrain (Grewal) brothers took turns courting favors from their dad by attacking like timber wolves on a crippled caribou. We did two short climbs and some singletrack, then did a 10-mile climb up into the stratosphere. At the top, it was cloudy; and when my eyes saw the rainbow jersey, my mind, in a 13,000-foot, oxygen-debt haze, couldn't remember what Gianni Bugno was doing in a mountain bike race. Luckily, Johnny said, "Hey Bobke," as I jogged up to him . . . and I remembered where I was. I bombed down the last, long descent to the finish, snorkeling though 8-foot-high weeds of a variety I've never seen before. Ned wasted all of us mere mortals, but lost the general classification by 1 second, because of some insane logistical fluke, to Rishi.

July 25

Mammoth Mountain, Grundig World Cup and NORBA national

Been hanging in Mammoth for a few days, visitin' my old haunts and cool brothers. The town is packed with mountain bikers, and the ski area has been turned into a huge BMX track. Did the course a few times this week, and it's very sweet. It is difficult, without being real technical, and the pumice is firm due to the recent rains. I really wanted to do well . . . and wound up 15th—not so bad.

The race started in a big pack, like a road race, but got strung way out on the first climb, and I was already suffering. By the second lap, I was creeping; but over the top of the third and last climb, my legs came around, and I flew past six guys for a decent place. As normal, above 10,000 feet altitude, Ned got out the big hammer and smashed us all about 5 feet underground.

August 5

Last night, after I got in from three weeks on the West Coast, John Parker called me and asked me to be downtown at 5:30 a.m. for a photo shoot, with the pros of Durango, for DARE. I said, "Hey, drugs saved my life, but I'll do it." Staggered out of bed and went to town, took the photos . . . and at least I got to eat at the "Durango Diner" while the green chili was still fresh. I hope the photos turn out, 'cause I won't be getting up this early again—unless the Pope comes to Durango and wants to see me.

August 22

Winter Park, NORBA national

Two days ago, I stopped in Leadville for lunch, and this morning it came back to haunt me. Suffice it to say, my chamois will never be the same. Tried to warm up, but all I could do was ride to the start and sit next to it for an hour, until we lined up. This was a brutal course, and I was shelled directly. I still wanted to finish, though, and managed to get around the course. I was so wasted, I fell three times on the last descent. The last time I fell, I was going to give up, but I wanted to race tomorrow, so I finished, hoping to feel better in the point-to-point, stage-2 Tipperary Creek race. Rishi and Ned continued to battle, with Rishi hanging tough for the win. I guess Ned is now the overall leader in the NORBA National Series. Surprise, surprise. . . .

August 23

Tipperary Creek, stage 2

I felt better today, and we started pretty mellow for a change, on a dirt road, until we turned left onto the singletrack and straight up a decent hill. Due to all the rain in Colorado this summer, the course was pretty slick, but I kept cruising along behind a small group, biding my time . . . and, pow, we hit the finish about an hour before I expected . . . no worries. Drove a long, long way home, but at least stopped in the original Hard Rock Café in Empire, Colorado, where I could see the grim-faced ghosts of long-dead immigrant miners, who lived their lives under a zillion tons of granite.

August 29

NORBA finals, Durango

Ooohhh weeeee, baby, it is nice to race near my home for the first time in many, many moons. Been going over the course for about a month, and I know it well. Rode up the mountain pass to Purgatory, as a warm-up, and for the first time this season, I felt ready to race. I lined up on the far left in the front row, and after Rishi hooked the field, I was flying in 3rd spot, behind John Tomac and a raging Don Myrah. I got over the top really well, just behind Johnny and Ned—who'd fallen on the start line and was making an unbelievable comeback, even for him. I started down the hill and passed

Myrah, who had wickedly beefed and krieged his schluttlebain; so when the crowd saw me hanging tough on the next hill, they went beserk. I then passed Johnny T., who was fixing his chain—but I could mark his progress, which was *awesome,* by the roar of the crowd down the hill. We went over the top together, me totally stoked . . . then I flatted. I was in such deep shock. I couldn't even curse, and that is *deep.* I sat there shakin' my head in disbelief for a minute, then decided to finish anyway. I still felt pretty good, but couldn't get back in the top five, no way, and wound up in unlucky 13th. What is a biker to do but ride his Harley into town, buy a fifth of Hura Dura and get plastered, and cruise around with Tomes and Mrs. Tomes, looking for fist fights with BMX dickheads from Los Angeles at the dual-slalom races?

September 5

Vail World Cup final

I guess, until 1962, this was a most excellent sheep ranch, but now it is the jewel of the Rockies—gag me with a wool sweater. And if you have five dollars, you can buy a cup of coffee—sweet.

As a roadie, I always raced well in Vail no matter what my form was like. But in mountain biking, you can't sit in and hope your legs come around. Today, I felt like the walking wounded and broke my own personal record of five crashes, set on a stage of the 1986 Tour de France that finished in Pau. I was tied with my very own record going down the last hill, when a baby gopher looked at me funny, and I went over the bars . . . sheeeeittttt! The course was awesome and the most difficult this season. I finished okay, and wound up 19th overall for the Grundig series. I got called for random today ('cause I spewed hard core about dope and NORBA in the last issue of *Mountain Bike Action,* I think), so I cruise over to the control, which luckily was the First Aid room as well, so I got to piss in the cup and patch my bleeding shins at the same time . . . bonus! Ned, after killing us all again, was in the control trying to pee. Daryl Price was trying to pee also, after getting second . . . excellent. So I peed, patched, and split Vail . . . ASAP.

September 16

Bromont world's qualifier

All us cheese-eaters who aren't on the national teams, plus Gerhard "Zaddy" Zadrobilek ('cause he don't drink 7-Up), had to race today in order to race again on Saturday. I felt good and wound up in 8th. When you feel good, mountain bike racing is one sweet sport, but if you feel bad, bag 'em, man.

September 19

Bromont world championship

Lined up this morning in row 82, behind a sea of chomping-at-the-bit psycho killers, next to Tinker and ten rows in front of Zaddy. The course was pretty nice, really, but very hard to pass on if you were at the back. I suppose the format for the world's will continue to evolve, along with the sport, but that thought comes nowhere near placating the frustration I felt by the time I even got to the start line, when I was already 2 minutes down on the leaders. Anyway, I kept plugging away, trying to finish, when I broke my chain and bent my chain tool fumbling with it, in that sweet, trailside, lactic-acid crippling haze I've been living in this year. It was too far to walk the last lap and a half, so that was all she wrote for me. Jerkhard Sirdribbledick had probably the best race of all, finishing 4th after starting dead last and chasing the whole race. But if he'd won, I guess we'd never get to race a World Cup in the real mountains again. I went direct to Southern California, where I rented a V-8 T-Bird and blasted down the 405 from LAX at 130 mph, to the bike show at Anaheim. My season was over. . . .

CHAPTER 12

Euro' Trashed

Bobke Hits the Grundig Pain Trail

The 1993 Grundig World Cup circuit began with three races—in Spain, Italy and Belgium. After following the mountain bike trail around the Continent, your intrepid correspondent returned home with a backpack full of tall tales and lowlifes. But it all started a few days earlier, in Moab, Utah. . . .

April 17, 1993

Had a fun time today—watching all the mountain bike honchos blow sky-high chow after trying to chase me during a hard, 80-mile road race here in Moab. I warned them all not to before, but the Boyzzz will always be the Boyzzz. Last year, I botched my sprint miserably, but this year, I held on till the line and snocked 'em en da spurt (as they say in Flanders). I'm toasted, but I hope I feel all right tomorrow in the dirt.

April 18

Felt great today and was pepperin' the boyz, until I flatted. I made a lame change and got going after the whole field went by. I couldn't decide if I should chase or noodle it in. Finally, I decided to chase—and moved back up into 3rd. Man, oh man, what a sport. I was flipped, clipped, tripped, and dipped in Utah shit, but stoked to have decent fitness before the Euro' World Cup races next week in España. Hasta la vista, bambina!

Euro' Trashed

April 20

Hate to leave the sweet San Juans on such a fine day, but the Euro' mud is calling me like a Beverly Hills salon to an aging screen star, and I've got to go. The Rockies (mountains, that is) looked sweet, all covered in ice-like God's snowcone, from the window of Mesa Scareways Vomit Comet Express to Denver. The flight to Washington, D.C., was nice, and I just began to doze off . . . when this manic-depressive ex-marine sat down next to me and grilled me for 3 hours about illegal aliens, Oakley sunglasses, Frisco Choppers, the effects of napalm, and Nancy Sinatra. Finally, I looked at him straight and said, "You look just like Charles Manson" (first thing I said the whole flight, and I swear he looked just like Charlie—without the swastika carved between his eyes). He kept right on ranting, so I put Queen Ida and the Bon Temps Zydeco Band on my Walkman and was instantly transported from the Ho Chi Minh Trail to the joyous Mardi Gras-colored, gumbo-flavored streets of pre-Lent New Orleans. The flight to Spain was excellent, because I got a row of seats to myself and hit the hay, while Ned chased his son all over the plane.

Landed in Madrid and fell asleep while waiting for my connection to Barcelona. Lucky for me, two sisters—about 100 years old each—decided to have a screaming match, inches from my jet-lagged head, and I woke up just in time to make my flight. The Emperor of Ghent, Luc "the Drifter" Eysermans, picked me up at the airport and we split to the race site. Met Johnny T. and did a lap of next Sunday's World Cup course. I was in a total 8-hour-time-change haze of jet lag, but managed not to kill myself.

April 23

Was it Johnny Cash who said, "Right around the corner, there is heartache"? Or was it Dante Aligheri? I don't know, but this week was breezing by just as sweet as deep-fried molasses, until I came flying around a blind downhill off-camber corner of the race course and creamed into two teenage-mutant-Spaniard, moped-riding buttheads. I have never in my life been in a rage that was beyond my rational thought—until that moment. But after daily doing the course, which is pretty technical, without falling, I went full ballistic at these two kids who caused me to eat it on the last practice lap I planned to do before the race. I tore big chunks of skin off my elbow and hip in the crash, then I tore some more skin off my knuckles, as I smashed my fists onto the boys' full-face helmets. I picked up their moped and chucked it off the ridge into the trees, and began shaking them by the throat until I ran out of rage . . . and I was positive they would never ride a moped down another World Cup race course again. In normal Euro' fashion, *all* the bikers arrived today, and when me and J.T. strolled down to dinner, they all turned and stared as we walked into the restaurant. Sheezzus, these Philistines have no shame.

April 25

World Cup day

Great Gosh Almighty, I took ten giant steps backward today. Be it jet lag, or overtraining, or bad food, or I don't know what, today I couldn't pedal through a warm dysentery turd to save my life. After breakfast, the rain that had been falling all night finally stopped. Johnny and I got on our bikes to ride the 20 km to the race site as a warm-up. Right from the moment I straddled my bike, I fell off, and even though the rain transformed the course into a running-and-slide race, I still felt like hell. I felt even worse due to the 30,000 *possessed* Spanish fans in attendance, who saw me roachin' off the back in the smoking section. Daryl P. rode really well and came from behind to finish 3rd. Frishy had no trouble in killing all. Juli F. burned the frauleins' race village down to the ground like a marauding Hun. I consoled myself with thoughts of sunny Italian days and mounds of fine pasta. . . .

Euro' Trashed

April 26

Loaded into some Euro' jet filled with the scum of the Earth (Eurojet trash), and prayed all the way to Milan that God would not strike us down. When we got to the baggage terminal, a strung-out-on-heroin German Shepherd stuck his nose in my crotch, so I bent down to pet him, hoping he wouldn't bite my privates off. The guard went ape and I told him the SPCA had a warrant out for his arrest. He didn't like that, and went through all of my bags and then all those of Kris Otter, who just happened to be standing next to me. For some reason, I always get dunked stern to stern in the trouble trough, every freakin' time I go through Linate Airport. What is Durango jet trash to do but drink five cappuccinos laced with Frangelico, bro? Since it was 10 a.m., the barman looked at me dubiously. I assured him I was sober half the time. The crew, me, J.T., Bobo G., and Luc the Drifter loaded up the van and split for Bassano del Grappa, for the next World Cup race.

April 30

I guess Zaddy didn't care for my criticism of his racing-at-the-sea-level-only ideas and, when I went to pick up my numbers today, Sirdribbledick starts spewing malarkey: "A bad mountain biker is writing shit about a good mountain biker!" I replied, "Jerkhard, you better choose your next words carefully." I was ready to hit him as hard as I could and see what happened to his head. But we both chilled, and I hope he realizes that I'm one of the few guys who actually likes him.

J.T. and I went to the managers' meeting with the UCI officials for grins. I can't remember one single thing that was said, so I guess either my brain is mush or they didn't say jack. Then, I went on this photo shoot and interview with some Italian journalist. One of my stone bros from the road, Stefano Guiliani, is also racing for Pro-Flex, and he smoothed things out in my jangled brain as we stood out in the rain looking for a suitable backdrop for photos. Giuli' turned a possibly lame day into a hell of a lot of fun. Riding back to the hotel, saw Rishi shooting hoops, so I had to stop and cream him—15-2 in one-on-one, after he waxed me in horse, H to H-O-R-S-E. Good Lord.

May 1

Bassano del Grappa World Cup qualifier

Unless you are in the top 50 on World Cup points, you have to do these qualifying races the day before and be in the top 80 or so on time—out of about 1,000 guys trying to qualify for tomorrow's main event. The qualifiers are fast, hard and dangerous . . . and just the thing you need before a World Cup race. So since I blew chow last Sunday, I lined up with 250 madmen in the heat and sprinted off the line for turn one, avoiding a huge pileup. I raced near the front and qualified okay. I hope I can recover by tomorrow, for some more sweet madness.

☆ ☆ ☆

Feeling yesterday's efforts in my legs, which were hard as wood as I warmed up—until I wrecked into the wall of a dang cemetery, due to pilot error.

May 2

Bassano del Grappa World Cup

Feeling yesterday's efforts in my legs, which were hard as wood as I warmed up—until I wrecked into the wall of a dang cemetery, due to pilot error. I suppose the race started fast, but I wouldn't know, since from the back of the pack, I could only walk up all the climbs on the first lap—even standing in place, at times, waiting for the pack to move. Meanwhile, Mike Kluge, Frish, J.T., and Daniele Bruschi were down the descent, battling it out across the flats. I am not easily bummed, but had to frown watching the leaders about 3 minutes ahead before I took *one* pedal stroke—ouch, harsh toke.

Anyway, I felt pretty good today and was stoked to be able to make forward progress throughout the race. Mike "Where's my blow dryer" Kluge *hurt* all—including Tommy F. and local hero D. Bruschi—for a fine win. Juli F. worked the women over again.

Feeling a bit homesick, the crew, plus Wild Bill Woodul, went in search of hamburgers and Budweiser for dinner, not an easy task in Italy. Since the restaurant we found with burgers (no Bud, ouch) wasn't open yet, we all went to a café in the piazza for a cappuccino, to kill time. We were enjoying a fine evening—shootin' the breeze, just standing in the town piazza waiting for dinner—when the village idiot looked straight at me and let loose with a blood-curdling scream, silencing the whole square full of locals. Pointing a filthy, bloated finger at me, he continued yelling at the top of his lungs, even attracting the attention of the police. My lactic-acid-laden brain was struggling to comprehend this bizarre scene, so I motioned for him to come closer. By now, everyone was watching what this confrontation between an obviously *very* disturbed old man and a lanky, dressed-from-head-to-toe-in-jet-black foreigner would lead to. I motioned again and said, "Come here," in Italian. He staggered over and in twisted Veneto dialect said, "You are afraid of me." I looked at his rotten black-to-the-roots teeth and said in nasty peloton dialect, "Not one freakin' bit," and stepped up ready to start swinging. Just then, the church bells tolled for supper time, so we split that strange scene for dinner—my homies shakin' their heads with bellies full of hunger, me shakin' my head with a belly full of post-adrenaline-rush acid.

May 4

Chillin' a few days extra here in pastaland, so all the slum lords of Durango went bikin' up Cima Grappa, a giant hill behind Bassano. About halfway up, the skies poured rain on us, and we got under a canopy to wait it out. After 10 minutes, it was still hammering down, so we decided to get a cappuccino in the local café. I spot two skinny Freds coming up the hill—decked out in Lampre gear, just like every other Italian, wanting to look like Maurizio Fondriest. I turn around to cross the street heading for the café when the Freds start yelling, "Bobo!" I was dipped in pesto when Mau Mau himself and Marco Zen stopped to say "hi." We all drank a cap in the café, and I introduced Ned and Daryl, who were gaping in wonder that their own homie Bobke would know honcho No. 1 in Europe. Mau said, "I had to ride halfway up Cima Grappa, just to see Bob Roll," and they split. I was stoked to see Mau and Marco, but sad not to be hanging with my road bros. Ned goes, "Why were they so happy to see you?" I said, "Well, it's kind of a long story. . . ."

May 5

Flew to Belgium and slotted into a sweet castle near Houffalize, drank Trappiste beer and ate wild boar for dinner, and fell asleep floating down the Mississippi, as John Lee Hooker and Sally Mae broke each other's hearts.

May 8

Belgium World Cup qualifier

Once again, I lined up with the boys for a rugged race, a day before the World Cup race. The course here is about a 45-minute loop, full of roots, rocks, and no reggae, but lots of hills, thrills—and, for me, spills. I beefed it so many times I lost count (I wish my skin could also). I felt so lame on the first lap that even though I felt better on the second, I still missed the final. This race was so hard, it would have been very difficult to do well tomorrow, anyway. But as Johnny T. says, "That is just the deal." And as Sean Y. says, "Just have to lump it."

Euro' Trashed

Drove up to Brussels for a meeting with all the Pro-Flex chiefs, and got to spy some of next year's rigs. This trip flew by, and soon I'll be 37,000 feet above the Atlantic going home—and I'm looking forward to fighting jet lag again and getting dropped on a different continent. Europe has put me in the hurt-locker before and thrown away the key, but Harry Houdini ain't got nothing on me.

THE CAST

Ned = Ned Overend

Johnny T. = John Tomac

Daryl P. = Daryl Price

Frishy = Frish = Tommy F. = Thomas Frischknecht

Juli F. = Juli Furtado

Bobo G. = Bob Gregorio (mechanic)

Zaddy = Gerhard Zadrobilek

Rishi = Rishi Grewal

D. Bruschi = Daniele Bruschi

Sean Y. = Sean Yates

Kris Otter = Kris Oetter

CHAPTER 13

Dream Season

May 20, 1993

Woke up early for flight to Big Bear, California, for first NORBA national. Due to the fickle nature of thermal storms above the Rocky Mountains, it is better to take the Vomit Comet flight from Durango to Denver early in the day, or get ready to bounce. I don't mind a little bouncin', but disappearing into a jet-black cloud 40,000 feet tall filled with millions of tons of electrical energy can give any sane person pause. But today all was "fine and mellow," as Billie Holiday might have sung on TV in the late 1950s. When I got to Ontario, California, I rented a large gas guzzler from Detroit, Michigan, and started blastin' down the nearest freeway at 115 mph. After an hour or so, I realized I had no idea where the hell I was or where Big Bear was located. So I took the next exit and found I was in Redlands right on the road to Big Bear . . . bonus. When I got to the venue at the ski area, it was very still and sorrowful. Normally, on Thursday before a NORBA national, the venue is jumpin', especially in California; but due to Leapin' Charlie Litsky's passing, the atmosphere was quiet and subdued. The sport won't be as good without Charlie. I rode a lap of the course real slow and melancholy.

Dream Season

May 21

Woke up early feeling like a mule kicked me in the kidneys. Hobbled over the the nearest diner and had a reasonable carbo breakfast of pancakes, oatmeal, French toast, and a waffle. Went over to ski area and rode a lap of the course—which is a bit different from last year, but still a gas. I ate lunch, then did another lap slow and easy. Sometimes I ride for hours trying to figure out where everyone I met was coming from and how I fit into the scheme of things. Today, I just did some miles, my brain too numb for travel and years of suffering to give a crap—no brain, no pain, I guess.

May 22

Lucid dreams careened through my head all night—about forgetting my cycling shoes, helmet, wheels, and number plate, and showing up at the start line naked from the waist down. Woke up in a sweat with a sore throat, but with my shorts on. I ate oatmeal and bacon for breakfast and took a 2-hour warm-up, listening to the Pogues on my Walkman. Got to the start line ready to rock. After an exhilarating moment of noise for Charlie Litsky, the starting gun went *Pow!* The Grewals got a flying start and we all

☆ ☆ ☆

Lucid dreams careened through my head all night—about forgetting my cycling shoes, helmet, wheels, and number plate, and showing up at the start line naked from the waist down.

sprinted up the start-lap hill. Ouch! We came past the start area after about 5 minutes and then went out onto the course for three long, hard laps.

Wiensy, Tinker, and Rishi broke away on the first climb. The rest of us did our best not to detonate, as the tempo was very fast. I hung in the top ten pretty well and was engulfed by a cloud of black dust as me and J.T. diced on the first descent. Johnny was flying, but I backed off 'cause I couldn't see jack. I kept cruisin' until I felt a bonk comin' on during the last climb. I was in 9th until Jeet G. came flaming past me. I could barely get down the last hill. When you bonk, even the most rudimentary procedures become difficult, but I hung on all right to finish 10th. Then I sat down on the grass about 2 feet past the finish line and couldn't move for an hour. Rest period over, I went to see the Shimano kids' race and had a great time instructing them, giving out medals, and signing some autographs. . . . Then I went to the media center for the results, so I could leave a message on my 900 number, then went out for Mexican food with the whole peloton—including Dave W., who worked us over today like precious metal during the Bronze Age. Then I got back in my Detroit bucket of gas-guzzlin' bolts and split for L.A., so I won't miss my early flight home tomorrow. Going home to see my baby, as Alvin Lee might sing.

> ★ ★ ★
>
> **I got back in my Detroit bucket of gas-guzzlin' bolts and split for L.A., so I won't miss my early flight home tomorrow. Going home to see my baby, as Alvin Lee might sing.**

May 28

Have been waylaid by some wicked virus and just layin' in bed since Big Bear. Tried to get up and smoke out the aches, but I passed out in the bathroom and crashed my head through the door, so I'll be layin' low for a while. Can't wait to lose my fitness and start from scratch. Oh boy.

June 10

Flew to Indiana with J.T. today for Bloomington NORBA. On the drive to venue, we stopped at the hometown of John Wooden (the nine-time NCAA champion basketball coach). We ate chicken fried steak and mashed potatoes under the gaze of Lou Alcindor (a.k.a. Kareem Abdul-Jabbar). We got to "Ski World" and did a lap of the "race" course.

June 11
Right on schedule, the monsoon hit Bloomington today and turned the course into a nightmare of retribution by an angry God for a life of sin.

June 12
Brought my mountain bike with me out here, but would have been better served by running shoes and a rain hat. I started the race well and bombed down the first hill, scattering spectators and sliding all over. On the next hill, we all had to dismount and run up. I got passed by half the field, and the other half got past me on the next run-up. I *never* voluntarily drop out, but this race was so frustrating I came very close today. Anyway, I finished up and Johnny T. roosted mud in all our mugs. I hope no NORBA officials ask me what I thought of this race, 'cause I'm trying to cut down on cursing.

June 17
Flew to Burlington, Vermont, and thumbed a ride to Mount Snow with fellow scribe Marti S. of Smello Snooze. The weather was perfect—clear, cool, and dry. Traveled all day and into the night and didn't arrive until midnight. Some journalists from Great Britain were waiting for me, and we did an interview from my hotel room, which was fun. Drank some tea and hit the hay like a thousand anvils.

June 18
This course is, uhh, challenging to say the least. And as usual, the rain came right on time for the race. Since it's way too simple to have any sort of *alternate* course, we just dove right into a very slippery and treacherous course.

The climbs were reasonable and rideable for the most part, but the descending through the woods was sketchy. The rains turned the already tricky roots and rocks into slimy skin peelers. I went pretty well through the woods, but traversing this off-camber track across an open field, I tanked into a pile of rocks and landed square on my kneecap, ouch! I got up slowly and kept going. Actually, I got faster as the race wore on and managed to make some World Cup points. Thomas F. put the hurt to everyone—on terrain he is awesome at riding. He is second to none at honching. All in all, I thought this was a good race, even though I'm still praying for the sun.

June 20

Stayin' in Mount Snow for another day, so I went to watch the downhill in a *pouring* rain storm, and saw about 90 percent of the racers come in with a flat, or two flats, or not come in at all.

June 21

Stayed over last night here in Burlington, Vermont, "you know it," to hang out with this tall, skinhead prison guard in Oakleys; Billy T., me, Johnny T., Daryl P., Pat Mac, and Travis B. all went to the local bike-museum shop and then to Catamount Nordic Ski Area for the Monday night mountain bike training race. This totally cool ski area is an oasis of nature right in the middle of suburban subdivision hell. The race was a blast, and hundreds of mountain bikers from all over showed up to race and hang out with J.T. After the race, all of Johnny's fans lined up to get photos from him. I had a few of my own fans, but they brought me home-brewed beer . . . *sweeett!*

June 23

On the drive to Quebec yesterday, I must've ate something poisonous, 'cause I was up all night with diarrhea . . . yuck. I guess there was some obstruction in my intestines and all the food I had for dinner just sat in my belly festering. Then at 1 a.m., it all came blowing out like a fire hydrant full of liquid shit. Anyway, I felt much better afterward.

June 27

Have been feeling stronger and stronger each day this week and started today's race in Mont-Ste.-Anne pretty well. I figured it was going to be a long race, so I went easy the first lap, but still managed to move up through the field aways. I began to work it and let it fly on the descents, and moved up into the top thirty or so, and I was cruisin', feeling good. Then, right in the feed zone, the derailleur blew up and my chain backed out of the bottom of the pulley cage. I sat there looking at the mess and I couldn't ever figure out what happened before twenty

☆ ☆ ☆

Only the statuesque blond looks of Wiensy captured the hearts of the crowd, and he won "Miss W.C. Mont-Ste.-Anne." Not to take anything away from Dave, but that is one contest I was happy not to win.

guys passed me. I could barely yank it back in the cage, but got going again. Then the dang chain broke at the top of the next hill. I fixed that and finished up totally bummed in 47th. Sheeeeitt!!

June has not been a good month for Bobke. June, however, has been a *great* month for Tinker, and he dropped Frishy to finish by himself and win a long-overdue World Cup race.

After the event, there was a huge banquet and a "beauty contest." The organizers asked Zaddy, Dave W., Stickman, K. Otter, Thomas F., Paul Watson, Joshua Klein, and me to be the "judges." Like morons, we all said okay. Except we were the contestants and looked absolutely hideous as women. Only the statuesque blond looks of Wiensy captured the hearts of the crowd, and he won "Miss W.C. Mont-Ste.-Anne." Not to take anything away from Dave, but that is one contest I was happy not to win.

Now, just Burlington-Chicago, Chicago-Denver and Denver-Durango to get back to my honey and the sweet Southwest. . . .

CAST IN ORDER OF APPEARANCE

Wiensy (or Dave W.) = Dave Wiens

Tinker = Tinker Juarez

Rishi = Rishi Grewal

J.T. (or Johnny T.) = John Tomac

Billy T. = Billy Treacy

Jeet G. = Ranjeet Grewal

Marti S. = Marti Stephens of *VeloNews*

Tomas F. (or Frishy) = Thomas Frischknecht

Dary = Daryl Price

Pat Mac = Pat MacIllvain

Travis B. = Travis Brown

Zaddy = Gerhard Zadrobilek

Stickman = Craig Glaspell

K. Otter = Kris Oetter

CHAPTER 14

Nerves + Neurosis

July 9, 1993

After a mellow 4-hour road ride, me, my frau, and bro' Kris Oetter split in Schralf Mobile for Crested Butte and this weekend's Fat Tire Fest. I was blastin' over the passes, drivin' like a fool as usual, to the distress of my wife and the Winnebago Armada that clogs up the highways around here every summer. Red Mountain Pass, retirees driving motor homes, and psycho bikers on a mission from God just don't mix that well. But we survived and arrived at midnight to sleepy C.B., Colorado, without doing too much damage—except to my eardrums from my wife yelling at me to "slow down or else!"

July 10

Stage 1, Fat Tire Fest, Crested Butte

This morning, I woke up gasping for air at 10,000 feet above the sea. Then ate some cakes and eggs, brewed a doo, and chamoised up. Since this morning's stage was going to be an hour or so, I took a pretty good warm-up and did a few jumps to hopefully prevent full detonation in the race. The circuit is not real technical, but pretty hard with lots of corners and a pretty hard climb. The start was hectic, but I felt good, and rather inexplicably began to fly. With a few laps to go, I even took the lead. Albert Iten and I dueled for the last couple of laps, and he won and I wound up second. I was pleasantly surprised to be honchin' in the front, and a most excellent bonus was that my sweet frau saw the whole thing.

Rugged single-track time trial this evening. This 3.5-mile course is as brutally hard as it is scenically beautiful. It starts with a hard climb, then a blasting descent through the aspen trees—and they absolutely do not bend if you clip one with your shoulder, as I now have the bruises to prove. I started hard and was going well when I caught a root with my foot just before a stream, did a face plant in the water, and almost drowned. If Jehovah's Witnesses are right, and they replay a film of your life when you die, I hope the Great Editor in the Sky leaves that scene out. Anyway, I finished up okay and cruised back to the hotel gazing at God's face etched into the Rocky Mountains by the Power of the Holy Spirit. I tried to get some results, but they were screwed up beyond reality—and even though a couple of guys passed Wiensy, he still won. That is some kind of local clout.

July 11

Stage 3, Cross-Country Fat Tire Fest

In 1992, this was probably the most epic mountain bike race I had ever done. It was an amazing trek through the gigantic mountains, approaching 13,000 feet at one point. But due to the heavy snows last winter, we had an alternate route that seemed less difficult on the map—*wrong*. Good Lord, what a gnarly race! Four full hours of rugged singletrack and high-altitude torture. The stage started with a long climb at 9 a.m., *ouch!* Then out to Gothic and about ten of us were left in the front. Wiensy jumped hard out of the blue, just in time for the singletrack that would last the next 3 hours. The course was up for 3 to 5 kilometers, then down steep, rough, twisty singletrack for 3 to 5 kilometers, and on and on for eternity. We crossed a butt-cold river twice and literally froze ass, as the water was about that deep. Having learned my lesson yesterday, I ran the streams. As an added bonus, the last 10 miles were straight up. I hung out in the top five for the first 3 hours, but began to bonk and started seeing people and things that didn't exist. I finished up all right and felt pretty stoked about the whole weekend. We split for Ouray to soak in the mineral baths, and I drove like a madman, even though I told myself to chill about one thousand times. Every time I get behind that steering wheel, I just can't get my mind right.

July 15

Commuting to Vail for this weekend's World Cup and NORBA national races, my frau and I went the back route over Coal Bank, Red Mountain, and McClure passes. For once in my life, I left my lead foot at home and Chiara didn't have to yell at me—well, not for my driving at least.

July 16

A *massive* pile of bikers from all over creation have descended on this former sheep ranch and turned this tourist trap into biker heaven. Woke up early and was checking out the village from my hotel when I saw an old Swiss friend, Pascal Ducrot, and yelled "good morning" to him. He looked up to wave and krieged into two fur-decked, Texan ex-cheerleaders, dripping with gold. Poor Pascal was on his butt in non-comprehending shock while the Vail-vacationing, credit-card-toting princesses lambasted him in gutter drawl, their beehive hairdos quivering with rage. Oh man, I tried to feel sorry for Pascal, but I was laughing too hard. I had a bagel and a croissant and a cup of tea for breakfast at the local bean-extraction shop . . . and split for a lap of the World Cup's most rugged venue.

July 17

Vail World Cup and NORBA national

This is probably the year's most difficult course. Add the fact that the race is about 8,000 feet up in the sky and you get some wasted bikers by day's end. I was gasping for breath from the start, and was as spastic as a Devo guitar solo until the last lap—when I felt better and passed about thirty guys. Beatnick Weeble didn't fall down and, rather amazingly for a lowland 'cross honcho, creamed everyone.

As usual, the race started fast and the first lap was a dust cloud of pain and desperation, as Bailey's Bail-Out became clogged with fallen bikers seeking praise from the assembled crash fans. I ran it and almost twisted my ankle, but that would have been better than eating shit in front of every cameraman and foaming-at-the-mouth ghoul of over-the-bars glory. I crashed about every other mile in 1992, so

☆ ☆ ☆

I was gasping for breath from the start, and was as spastic as a Devo guitar solo until the last lap . . .

I kind of went for control and didn't lose any more skin this year. After feeling so strong last week in Crested Butte, I hoped to go a whole lot better here, but in a nutshell: That's bikin'. Gave the fair motorists of Colorado a break and let my wife drive home—I was so wasted. I couldn't see straight enough to drive anyway.

July 21

Picked up Johnny T. early at his house and drove to the La Plata airport. J.T. had a big pair of frequent-flier first-class upgrades and most excellently styled me out with one. We were dressed in denim and big cowboy hats, and we had a great time telling stories about road racing in Europe . . . but not missing the life one iota. But I won't be flying first class again because

Wiensy, who flew coach on the same flight, massacred us all two days later. Must have been them sweet stale pretzels you get in coach.

July 22

Pedaled easy down to the Devil's Postpile National Monument. Thank God there is now a shuttle down there instead of unlimited cretin access for no dollars down, no interest 'til March, and no penalties for unexamined abuse of God's blue sky and green valleys. It felt good to ride on a beautiful scenic road and not breath fumes. *Real good.*

July 23

Mammoth World Cup and NORBA national

This used to be an insanely hard race, but I guess not hard enough, so they added a pair of steep, little leg-breaking climbs preceded by rough U-turn corners. Actually, I shouldn't complain, because the extra hills unhinged Bruschi, Ned, and Zaddy . . . and I squeaked by them on the last lap to wind up 20th. I started well and caught the second group on the long climb after lining up last on the grid. Feeling pretty strong, I kept plugging away, passin' guys who were blowing up from starting too fast. Here in Mammoth, if you bonk, you lose about thirty places—before you can say Coke and a Snickers, please. But I timed my effort pretty well and finished without crashing or bonking or flatting. After I got the results for my 900 number, I split the venue high on suffering and traced prayers on the roof of my mouth with my tongue spelling out the Rosary giving thanks. I was already packed and had split town to Reno before *Big Bad Dave* had collected the winner's bouquet.

August 5

Whoa, had the gnarliest flight I've had for a long time today. We left Durango at 2 p.m. (whoops) and for 30 minutes it was rough, but not too bad. Then we disappeared into some dark, very ominous clouds. Hailstones began to pummel the roof and sounded like a billion marbles being fired point-blank at an aluminum casket as it was being lowered into the grave. Lightning illuminated the cabin, giving quick glimpses of frequent fliers filling barf bags. I pride myself on having a cast-iron gut, but the violent pitches combined with the stench of vomit made me so nauseous I almost lost the Kitchen Sink omelet I ate at the "Durango Diner" this morning. By the time we touched down at Denver's Stapleton Airport, I was green, and it took me a while to regain my equilibrium. . . . The flight to Chicago was like lowridin' a Cadillac on a brand new stretch of freeway listening to Sarah Vaughn after drinking four extremely dry martinis. I'm talkin' smooth. Then got a late puddle-jumper to Traverse City, Michigan, for Saturday's NORBA final.

August 6

Well, figuring the Traverse City NORBA was in Traverse City, I had to drive an hour and change to Schuss Mountain where the actual venue was. Shit, I love driving so much, too. Anyway, it was raining when I got there and I did a few laps. The sandy soil absorbed most of the rainwater and the course was fun— with rolling hills and only a few very silly man-made log piles. . . . I drove back to my hotel and ate spaghetti alone, thinking about tomorrow's race.

August 7

Nice sunny day driving to the venue. I parked right up front next to the expo and start-finish, telling the parking attendant I was the roto-rooter man and shit was going to spill out of every toilet around if he didn't get out of my way. Felt bad about fibbing until I saw the sea of cars stretching to the horizon. Which made me realize that NORBA races have very little to do with real mountain biking anymore. All the bikers were dashing about with last-minute details, but I took my bike over to Gravy nice and slow, so he could lay his hands on it. After Bobo G or Gravy so much as *look* at my bike, I feel calm and ready to race.

Johnny T. pulled up in his van and was greeted by about 1,000 local relatives. There were relatives he didn't know he had. I warmed up well on sandy back roads and felt pretty loose toein' the start line. The start was even faster than the wicked starts of today's mountain biking, but I felt okay and was cruisin'. Mark Howe then decided he had to get around me on a descent just before a sharp turn—as if I'm some lame-ass who can't slide knobbies around a loose corner. He proceeded to beef it as his front wheel crossed up and washed out, and I creamed into his prostrate body going over the bars myself. I frowned heavily, but got up pretty quick and found my rhythm and was closing on the leaders pretty well. I was getting excited about finally feeling good and went way too fast on the descent through the woods—going off course and launching through the trees. Luckily, I missed all the trees, but my bike didn't and bent my front rim. I kept racing, but the brake shoe rubbing on the sidewall finally blew out my tire. I thought about booting it with pine needles, but my hands were shaking too much to tie my shoes, let alone do a hippie survival maneuver during a race. I was totally bummed walkin' back to the finish. Travis T. Brown is having a b-day party at some bowling alley, and if I can find a designated driver, I'm gonna get wasted on billiards, bowling, and beer.

CAST

Wiensy, Big Bad Dave = Dave Wiens	**Ned = Ned Overend**
Beatnick Weeble = Beat Wabel	**Zaddy = Gerhard Zadrobilek**
Johnny T., J.T. = John Tomac	**Gravy = Steve Gravinites**
Bruschi = Daniele Bruschi	**Bobo G = Bob Gregorio**

Rhythm is a Racer

In mountain bike racing, momentum is crucial. Your rhythm through-out the race dictates your placing; maintaining an efficient tempo is the difference between winning and losing. In fact, how well you do each weekend comes down to your rhythm. And the rhythm of the race begins at home.

Monday

Monday for me means recovery. Lots of eating, sleeping, and reflecting on the race that weekend. Also, Monday is for planning out the week's train-ing, travel, diet, rest—and any commitments to my sponsors. And finally, Monday is report-to-the-team day. If I've raced well, I can't wait to call the team; but if the race was bad, I don't like Mondays.

Tuesday

Tuesdays are my day alone. I set no schedule for anything except training. I try to do my hardest training day on Tuesdays—the day on which I am most recovered from the previous race, and hopefully will have time to recover before the race on the next weekend. I like to do a warm-up, followed by a hard 2-hour session reflecting the next race—with sustained climbing to prepare for western races like Mammoth or Vail, or intervals of 3 to 5 minutes to prepare for races with shorter climbs, like Mount Snow and Traverse City. The rest of Tuesday is for lying on the couch and searching the TV dial for "Beverly Hillbillies" reruns.

Wednesday

The main consideration for me on Wednesday is to be packed. Both my suitcase and mountain bike have to be ready for Thursday's flight, and I need to try to get it all done today, so on flight day I'm not running all over the place forgetting gear and getting pissed. I have, over the years, learned exactly what is essential and what is dead weight. My suitcase has two sides. One side is for civvies and one side for team clothes.

Team clothes

4 pairs bib shorts	2 base-layer tank tops
3 short-sleeve jerseys	1 pair Time shoes
1 long-sleeve jersey	1 Giro helmet
1 team vest	3 pairs Oakleys
1 pair leg warmers	2 pairs long-finger gloves
1 pair arm warmers	1 pair short-finger gloves
4 pairs socks	

Personal clothes

3 pairs jeans (2 blue, 1 black)	1 sweater
1 pair Tony Lamas	1 jacket
1 pair sneakers	5 pairs socks
4 T-shirts (2 team, 1 Troy Lee, 1 H-D)	1 baseball cap
4 pairs undershorts	

Looks simple. It is, *now*—but it took a long time to get alchemized down to the essentials. On Wednesday, I also try to confirm all the reservations—like the flight, hotel, rental car, entry . . . because there are few things more damaging to my calm façade than lost reservations. Ouch!

Thursday

Flying to venue. Flying around the country all summer can wear you out as much or more than the races themselves, so I try to take a few steps to mitigate travel misery. I always pack plenty of fluids and drink constantly, because dehydration and flying go hand in hand. I also pack my race shoes and a team jersey, just in case they lose my luggage. Other essentials are a Walkman, tapes, and some reading material. I always dress in jeans, boots, T-shirt, and cowboy hat, with a jacket in carry-on baggage. Now, when I show up to the airport, I am ready to travel.

Living in Durango entails the microflight over the Rockies to Denver. From Denver, I try to get to the closest airport to the venue. This is not always very close and some driving usually follows every flight. I try to rent large, indestructible American cars, because dying in a car wreck on the way to a mountain bike race would require more delicate explanation to Saint Peter than I am capable of. So there I am at the venue. I try to do at least one lap of the course on Thursday to get a feeling for what the race will be like. I also pick up my numbers and race packet at registration, cruise around the venue, and say hi to all the boys. Now it's time to find the hotel, shower, and get some chow. After dinner, I am usually tired and nervous. That is a strange feeling, but I'm getting used to it and it has become part of the rhythm of the races.

Friday

Friday is for final adjustments to the mountain bike and some easy laps around the course. Friday is also for loading up on nutrition (my favorite part of the whole week). If you bonk in a mountain bike race, you are going to lose more places than a crippled gazelle running from a lion. So I try to eat as much as I can get down my throat—which sometimes is a lot. Also drinking enough to prevent dehydration is essential, *especially* at altitude. In between stuffing my face and lying down, I set out all my race gear: shoes, socks, shorts, jersey, warm-ups, gloves, helmet, Oakleys, and water bottles. I try to consume the most complex-carbos I can at dinner on Fridays. I generally seek out Italian restaurants void of massive quantities of bikers. This is sometimes difficult, especially in some of the towns in which NORBA hosts races. After dinner is bedtime. I am pretty keyed up, so sleep is often difficult, but dreaming is easy. Poetry runs through my brain all night, and usually it's filled with fear and loathing . . . like:

Low Grade Man

I can't handle my systems

> *Hell Hole*
>
> *Go Home*
>
> *No Home*

I am a cracked minded man.

Saturday

Race day. I like to be up 4 hours before the race and eat a reasonable breakfast: cakes with syrup, or oatmeal with a couple of eggs, some fruit, and tea. I like to finish breakfast 3 hours before the race and get my legs up for a few minutes before warming up. I do a long warm-up, gradually increasing my tempo, and after 1.5 hours, I'm usually ready to race. The staging area is a very nerve-wracking place, so the less time spent there the better. I try to stage just before they call my name, and cruise up to the line completely ready. Bang, the race always starts with the most violent acceleration, and finding a rhythm is difficult. Then, I settle into a rhythm that is just shy of blowing sky high and is usually excruciatingly painful. Still, reaching the finish line is very sweet. Most guys get tired from racing, but I get all jacked up and it takes awhile for me to calm down. A long while. But now it's time to pack it all up and head for the nearest airport.

Sunday

The downhillers are doing their stuff today, but the cross-country folks are 33,000 feet in the air, flying home. When I get back to Durango, my wife picks me up at the airport, and if I have won some money, we go out to dinner. If not, I eat humble pie at home. What a sweet life.

☆ ☆ ☆

The Watch

When I signed my first pro contract, I got two things: a passport and a wristwatch. I vowed to race until all the pages of my passport were filled with stamps (like Sidney Poitier's Virgil Tibbs in "In the Heat of the Night") or it had expired. In a lame attempt to expedite border crossings, most European countries no longer stamp your passport, and since mine doesn't expire for a couple of years, my original vow will give me an even decade as a pro. The wristwatch came from one of the team's co-sponsors. Not just any watch, but a TAG-Heuer titanium-and-gold piece of exquisite Swiss art.

When I look at the pre-EEC stamps on the pages of my passport, I can easily remember the places I've been and the races that brought me there. But looking at my watch reminds me of my physical presence at those places and races.

That wristwatch exploded off Tour de France prologue time trial ramps from Paris to Berlin. That watch saw my arms and legs turn blue and counted 12 beats of my heart for one sweep of the minute hand during blizzard Giro stages in the Dolomite mountains.

That watch's crystal face glistened with citric acid from the peels of blood oranges in desolate hilltop Sicilian towns, and mirrored the vision of my jagged teeth turned crimson from the juice of the orange. That watch ticked out moral time for the victims of the Mafia whose photos gazed at me from boarded-up windows of decimated family homes from Palermo to Catania, during Tour of Sicily stages. That watch signed on a thousand times in smoky Belgian cafés, as I cursed Columbus for stealing tobacco from the Indians, and wondered if the bonehead bikers had any idea whatsoever where tobacco comes from.

★ ★ ★

That watch's crystal face glistened with citric acid from the peels of blood oranges in desolate hilltop Sicilian towns, and mirrored the vision of my jagged teeth turned crimson from the juice of the orange.

That watch shook hands with Eddy Merckx and Gino Bartali, and feasted from the floors of Rio Grande pueblo homes. It was splashed with holy water in Lourdes and measured out 1:57:00 by the second—in absolute terror—on a flight from Chicago to Denver, during a wicked thunder-and-lightning shower . . . while Richard M. Nixon sipped Shirley Temples in the first-class section.

In cycling, sponsors come and go and the jerseys change colors and names. Over the years, that watch passed from normal team swag into a rare living heirloom of suffering and deliverance. So this winter, when I lost my watch, I felt a sadness that made my bones ache, a sadness that hurt to the core.

On January 13, 1993, me and two local bros, Tio Cosa and Bobo G, went back-country snow boarding, high in the La Plata mountains. They wanted to carve some clandestine deep-powder turns, as far removed from mohawked skate punks on ice as possible. I wanted to improve my descending rhythm for the upcoming mountain bike season. But each 3-minute run

The Watch

entailed a 2-hour hike up the mountain ridge. The real Rocky Mountain winter snows had returned this year, and climbing the ridge to snowboard down required endless post-holing, even with snow shoes. I thought it was a perfect winter training day—not only developing descending technique, but offering the cardiovascular benefits of difficult power climbing. After the third run, snow had begun to fall again, and night was coming on, so we decided to bag it for the day and hike out to the highway.

When we got to the car and started to load up, I realized I had lost my bloody watch. I let out an anguished scream to the heavens, as I looked back on a million square acres of ice. Tio and Bobo said we would return in the spring when the snow melts and look for it. But in my dismay, I could only feel my negligence.

All winter, the snow continued to fall in the La Platas, burying that watch deeper and deeper into the ice. So much snow fell that a number of buildings collapsed in Durango—including one bread factory that almost killed Monty and Ivan, my local ski honcho bros, whose trailer got leveled, leaving two coffin-like cubes on either end, where they happened to be sleeping. I hoped my watch was in suspended animation, ticking away just as it had done from Oakland to Oostende . . . but I realized the chances of finding it were reduced to slim and none, with each waving of El Niño's moist wand. I continued my life as a biker while time continued its progress toward some divine end, each second measured by my watch buried under a billion cubic feet of frozen water, high in the La Plata Mountains.

I flew back east, crossing two-time zones to sign contracts and take photos at the end of January, and then out to California for races and a training camp. I went back to the ridge April 7, but the hill was still under 10 feet of snow. I went to Europe for a month, hoping the spring melt-off wouldn't carry my watch away downstream to some Anasazi grave at the bottom of Lake Powell.

Bobke II

When I got home from Europe, I was pretty tired as usual. Instead of hiking through the mountains looking for a watch, I would have preferred to sit on the couch eating green chili and watching "Beverly Hillbillies" reruns. But such was not my fate, and on Saturday, May 15, I set out again to try and find my watch. I pedaled down the Animas Valley through Durango, and up the long climb on Highway 160W toward the La Platas.

My wife, Chiara, met me on the highway, directly below the ridge we boarded on this winter, to help me look. I changed into some hiking boots and we began the hike up the ridge, trying to retrace last winter's ill-advised steps. As we crossed a grassy plain, I regained some hope, because it was easy to see every aspect of the ground. The initial hope was wiped out as we began the steep climb up the ridge. A forest of the thickest scrub oak enveloped us and tore at the exposed skin of our arms, legs, and faces. The winter snow pack, which made a relatively regular surface, had given way to a mangled mass of confusion. What looked like a smooth white sea this winter had boiled, avalanched, shifted, overgrown, plunged, and melted into an impossible maze of weeds, thorns, branches, mud, patchy snow, and stinking cow patties.

We navigated through this in a pathetic attempt to remember events now 5 months past, to find one small wristwatch that was getting smaller by the step. Try as I may to recall last winter's route, things had changed so much I began to doubt if I were even on the correct ridge . . . or in the same mountain range. I remembered some phone lines that were overhead when we boarded, and saw them on top of the ridge. By now, I figured the level top of the ridge was the only place on the whole hill I could exactly retrace my steps and have any hope of finding the watch. I climbed up the ridge top and began walking back and forth, but without success.

I started back down the hill almost killing myself—after slipping on an icy snow patch and accelerating to terminal velocity toward a drop-off, before being halted by a thorn-vine-wrapped scrub oak tree. "All right, that is it!" I cried aloud, and began to walk back to the car in anger and despair. I followed my footprints from that morning, back down to the highway, not ready to give up, but trying to be realistic.

And as the name St. Anthony lit up my mind, as I tried to remember the patron saint of all things lost, just as my wife pointed to a circling red-tail hawk above my head . . . there it was. Glistening like a diamond on a mountain of coal dust, my watch smiled up at me from a patch of snow. I let out a massive primal whoop, scaring Chiara, but *I just could not believe it.* I couldn't take my eyes off the watch—for fear of losing it again—and incredibly, it was keeping perfect Mountain Standard Time.

I pedaled home, edified for looking at a Goliath of doubt and slinging the giant to the ground, and humbled by not really knowing what I had until it was gone. I recommend that everyone keep a daily diary—so as the memory fades, you have a record to look back on—and never go back-country snowboarding with your favorite watch.

☆ ☆ ☆ ☆ ☆

PART II

☆ ☆ ☆ ☆ ☆

CHAPTER 17

The Sport According to Bobke

A is for the a**hole, the guy passing you in a car who spit, threw something, strafed, beeped, yelled, flipped the bird . . . and is the lowest form of scum on the earth. Cars break down—instant karma is a real bitch.

B is for the Butthole Surfers from Austin, Texas. One of Lance's favorite bands. Their song "Dust Devil" has massive feedback, enough to get you through a Tour stage.

C is for coffee. It's not just a beverage, it's a food group.

D is for descent. Why else would any sane person climb hills on bicycles?

E is for Eeklo. This tiny Belgian village has produced more Tour winners, classics conquerors, and world championships than all of China, India, Russia, and the United States combined.

F is for Fausto Coppi. After World War II, when cycling ruled all sports, Coppi was king.

G is for global warming. How else am I going to get in my winter training miles? Move to Los Angeles? Yeah right!

H is for heinous, like all the mountain bike races east of the Mississippi River.

I is for Italy, the greatest place to be a cyclist.

J is for Juli. Juliana Furtado, the queen bee of world mountain biking.

K is for kermesse working class, meat-and-potatoes bike racing for the Flemish masses.

L is for LeMond . . . 'nuff said.

M is for Missy and Mig. Opposite approach, same result. Only cycling has the scope to crown these two very different people as champions.

N is for NORBA. Slam 'em all you want, they are still the only game in town.

O is for off back, as in, "Oh shit, I'm off the back again!"

P is for pasta. In massive quantities. Originally from China, to Marco Polo to Europe to every cyclist on earth.

Q is for quick release, invented by Tullio Campagnolo, who is in heaven right now putting the finishing touches on God's gruppo.

R is for road rash, the ultimate tattoo for the biker clan.

S is for suspension. As far back in history as Leonardo Da Vinci, suspension had been taking the pressure off a cyclist's vital parts.

T is for the Tour de France. As it was in the beginning, is now, and forever shall be the ultimate bike race.

U is for Union Cycliste Internationale. You don't know them, but they know you. . . . Big Brother is watching.

V is for *VeloNews*, without which nobody would know shit.

W is for wheels. Like rain and sweet potatoes, wheels came from God. Heaven is filled with velodromes and singletrack. Kinda like Ghent and Crested Butte.

X is for x-ray. If you have been bikin' and haven't had an x-ray yet, you ain't going hard enough.

Y is for Yatesy. To know Sean Yates is to love Sean Yates.

Z is for Zapata. Zappy Espinosa is the last word in mountain biking.

BOBKE'S TEN COMMANDMENTS

I.

Thou shalt crash and look like a fool sooner or later.

II.

Thou shalt not touch thy front brake while negotiating
off-camber switchback turns.

III.

Thou shalt wear thy helmet every ride.

IV.

Thou shalt be thrashed, trashed, crashed, and smashed by someone
younger and stronger than you. (Absolution to Ned Overend.)

V.

Thou shalt pee in a cup eventually.

VI.

Thou shalt not covet thy neighbor's bike swag.

VII.

Thou shalt have your bike destroyed and your
luggage lost by the airlines.

VIII.

Thou shalt be screwed by one cycling federation or another.

IX.

Thou shalt be screamed at by one Grewal or another.

X.

Thou shalt not take the name of Eddy Merckx in vain.

CHAPTER 18

The "Water Hole" Revisited

NORBA's National Championship Series No. 3 will be held in Michigan at the Schuss Mountain Resort. Except for the occasional golf course blighting the landscape, this is a beautiful part of the country. The course we race on is challenging as well as fun. There are numerous hard climbs and tight single-track descents. All in all, it is a pretty fair course—except for the a man-made obstacle of questionable merit called the "Water Hole."

About halfway around the course we arrive at the Water Hole. The race organizers built a dirt mound, dug a hole right behind it, laid a plastic tarp in the hole, filled the hole with water, and put a few bales of hay in front of the trees that must be avoided upon landing the jump. "Did you do the jump?" "Did you do the jump?" "Did you do the jump?" About a thousand times a day you hear the same question.

Nobody wants to know how your training is going, how you did the previous weekend, how your family is. All anyone wants to know is, did you do the jump and are you going to do the jump in the race. The whole importance of the event as part of the NORBA NCS (as well as being the final Olympic Selection event this year) becomes overshadowed by a big hole in the ground. Days prior to the race, you will find hundreds of people milling around the jump. I'm not really sure why, but I suspect that everyone loitering there is hoping someone will crash and hurt themselves. Same scenario on race day. A few spectators scattered around the course, thousands of screaming fanatics at the jump.

The race directors, after much lobbying by a number of pros, have put in a bypass to the direct left of the jump, but pity the fool who uses it. Your efforts will go virtually unnoticed the rest of the course, and a massive collective "boo" will be your reward as you bypass the jump. I don't know about you, but 2 hours into a savage battle against the world's best mountain bikers, the last thing I want to hear is 5,000 to 10,000 hot dog-chewin', sun-basted Midwesterners booing my sorry non-jumpin' tired ass.

There is, however, something worse than getting booed at the Water Hole. It is missing the jump, crashing, and breaking bones. At the jump site, you are at least three or four big shots of morphine away from the nearest surgeon. Unless you are proficient at jumping, why risk injury and possibly ruining the rest of your season? But more importantly, why do the race directors feel this is a necessary part of their sport? Is a mountain bike cross-country race not exciting enough, as it follows the natural contours of the landscape? Will their spectators stay home and watch monster trucks and Wrestlemania on TV instead?" I doubt it. And why don't the downhillers get an obstacle such as a big jump over a water hole? I'll bet 99.9 percent of the downhillers would love a chance to show off their tremendous jumping abilities.

The confrontational and belligerent attitude taken by the race organizers during the pro cross-country race meeting had made a marginal situation worse in my mind. But what ices the cake for me is the quote from the race organizers' own race program from the 1995 edition, in an article aptly titled "The Water Hole": "The most spectacular crash occurred when a sport rider decided *not* to jump the water hole at the very last second and ended up completely submerged in the water with riders flying over him as he came up for a breath of air." No mention of numerous riders who skied the jump with aplomb and grace.

Hey, how about some burning hoops to jump through, or a few dozen land mines? Why not put some alligators in the water and *really* spice things up? A cross-country race should mean just that, cross-*country*. In the meantime, you can find me down at the local BMX track, practicing my jumps in a flame-retardant suit.

CHAPTER 19

One Heli Tour

In the unlikely event you are in an airplane crash, there is only one thing to do: pray. As a neo-pro 10 or so years ago, this thought never occurred to me. So every time I flew anywhere I was literally scared shitless. I mean, I couldn't shit for a day before or after any type of air travel. There was, however, one flight in particular that I anticipated with more fear than any other. It was a mountaintop airlift via a military helicopter climb in the Alps, just recently paved and called the Col de Granon. It went up a dead-end road barely the width of a small Peugeot. The only problem for the organizers was how to get everyone down the mountain after we finished. Volià, enter the French Air Force and a fleet of helicopters. That plan sat festering with dread in the back of my mind that entire Tour.

Stage 17 to the Col de Granon, starting in the Gap, was a typical beast. Right out of town, this Spanish-fly pain in the ass, Iñaki Gaston, started attacking like a lunatic. He attacked about 200 times—and each time the whole peloton chased him down. I became less and less happy and swore to strangle Gaston if I could ever get my hands on his neck. Mercifully, Gaston finally realized he would be chased every time, so he sat up. Just then, Edoardo Chozas, who was not a G.C. threat, launched off the front, never to be seen again until he was on the top step of the stage winner's podium.

Meanwhile, the peloton settled down to a mellow crawl as this big Dutchman, Gerrie Knetemann, told jokes in English, mostly poking fun at Greg. Knetemann called out to LeMond from halfway back in the peloton "Hey, Greg, how do you make a silly boy?" LeMond couldn't really hear and asked. "What?" Knetemann said, "Ask your daddy!" to the howling delight of all English-speaking riders. When you get into the third week of the Tour, third-grade humor becomes insanely funny. Then Knetemann yelled, "Hey, Greg, if you have six half-dollars, how many fifty-cent pieces do you have?" By now, LeMond was listening and trying to figure out the answer. As each second ticked by, the group laughed louder and louder. Just as Greg was about to answer, boom! There was a huge pileup.

I was on Knetemann's wheel as he wove a master's thread through the carnage of falling bodies. We had both nearly fallen nearly ten times, when a tiny escape path opened up. I darted through and saw Knetemann start to smile, anticipating a fine escape from impending doom. Pow! Out of the sky, in a full flying W, Alex Stieda landed flat on Knetemann's back. Knetemann screamed curses like a madman even as he fell. . . . Right then, I decided to pay more attention to the race than to Knetemann's jokes.

Our slow tempo, which gave Chozas a nice lead, was about to come to an end as the Col de Vars came into view. In no time we were flying along, with the Carrera and La Vie Claire teams setting a wicked tempo to move up their leaders—Zimmermann, and Hinault and LeMond, respectively—before the climb. I actually felt pretty good and had no trouble staying near the front. LeMond was also cruisin' along, looking strong and smooth. Hinault, on the other hand, was in obvious distress, pedaling ragged squares in the yellow jersey. The Col de Vars was steep and rugged, and the peloton splintered instantly on impact.

I felt really good, just floatin' on the pedals and hung near the front all the way up. Chozas still had a good lead as we started the day's second climb, the Col d'Izoard. Ouch! What a bitch! Straight up, with very little shade. The tempo was savage, guys blowing up everywhere, peeling off the front like gazelle flesh in a pride of lions. At the point when I thought the tempo could no way get harder, Zimmie attacked like a freak of nature. He nearly doubled the pace and shelled Hinault like the blitzkrieg. LeMond got on Zimmie's wheel, and I decided Hinault was going plenty fast enough for me. Over the top of Izoard in my group was Luc Roosen, J.P. Vandenbrande, Zootemelk in the rainbow jersey, and Hinault in the yellow.

Finally, the day's last climb, the Col de Granon. A massive *hors categorie* steep-ass ball-breaker. The French fans were foaming at the mouth, screaming for Hinault to try and catch LeMond. Knowing LeMond had dropped Hinault by staying with Zimmie, and fearing that he might gain enough time to get the yellow jersey, these fans seemed wine-bent and hell bound, as if their exhortations would propel Hinault up the mountain. My legs were beginning to cave in, and I sure as shit didn't need thousands of drunk Gallic sociopaths yelling obscenities in my face just because I came from the same country as LeMond . . . so I eased off the gas and rode my own tempo to the top and my waiting fate with the French military helicopter corps.

The top of the mountain looked more like a war zone than a bike race. Evac helicopters everywhere, TV crews, team personnel, police and motorcycles, and fans crammed every inch of non-official space—and just for a dramatic effect, a collapsed French racer, Joël Pelier, laid out right on the finish line.

I saw Shelley, waiting with cold drinks and our after-race bags. I grabbed my bag, put on a dry T-shirt and cap, and was immediately whisked to the nearest helicopter. I got the steps to board and nearly froze. From outside in the bright sun, I couldn't see into the helicopter. I almost turned around, but my joy at racing well in the day's mountains carried me up the steps. If we crashed, I was going out in a blaze of glory, I reasoned, in my fatigue-addled state of mind. The commotion in the finish area became a slow-motion drone ringing in my ears.

As my eyes adjusted to the darkness inside the 'copter, I saw that none other than Andrew Hampsten was seated directly across from me. "Whoa, Drew baby!" I practically jumped up at seeing a fellow American. "Andy, you slayed today," I exclaimed in glee. "Did you see LeMond crush these frog dweebs?" I asked.

Andy just kind of nodded, all subdued. As my eyes adjusted further, right next to Andy sat Greg LeMond, gloriously clad in yellow. "Whoa!!" I jumped up for real and grabbed LeMond by the shoulders, shaking him and screaming, "Greg, you beast! You got the yellow jersey, man! You're going to massacre these Philistines." I sat down and said, "I was climbin' with Hinault, and all the Frenchies were pissed that you dropped his sorry ass."

Just then, my eyes fully adjusted to the darkness and there sat Bernard Hinault himself. Oops. I could've crawled under my seat. "Hey Bernie, what's up?" was about all I could mumble. To make matters worse, the owner of the La Vie Claire team and one of France's biggest industrialists, Bernard Tapie, was sitting right next to Hinault. Tapie's script for Hinault to win his sixth Tour de France was about to be rewritten by LeMond.

But instead of pouring champagne and celebrating a major coup, Greg and Andy looked like they were at a funeral. I thought, well maybe I had better cool it and just fly off the mountain nice and easy.

One Heli Tour

The door was closed and 'copter blades started to howl. I looked straight at the drab olive wall and saw stenciled there in big white military letters, "Made in the USA." "All right, Tapie," I screamed, "you see this (pointing to the sign)? Made in the USA. Baby, everything is gonna be fine."

Tapie was not amused, but Greg, Andy, and me all started cracking up. Even Hinault cracked a little smile. We took off in a cloud of dust and the rest, as they say, was cycling history.

As you follow this year's Tour, remember, for every headline about the leaders, there are 100 everyday dramas about everyone else.

CHAPTER 20

Bobke's Back!

By popular demand, VeloNews *presented presented "Bobke's Corner" on a fairly regular basis beginning in 1997. This opening selection consists of two, typically irreverent offerings critical of the modern world's gas-guzzling ethos. Oh, and by the way, Bobke does go to church every Sunday. . . .*

The Lord's Prayer, Reviewed

Our dollar who art in Heaven,

Hallowed be thy spending power.

Thy OPEC come,

Thy will be sold,

On Earth as it is in the ozone.

Give us this day our daily

tankful of gas, and forgive

us our emissions as we

forgive those who kill for Exxon.

Lead us not into Chapter 11,

But deliver us from Greenpeace.

　　　　　　　　—Ahhem

Hail Mary, Revisited '97

Hail Mary full of smog,

the car dealers are with you.

Blessed art thou amongst

gas-producing nations,

and blessed is the fruit

of thy womb, fossil fuels.

Holy Benzine, Mother of

Carbon Monoxide, pray for

us cyclists now and at the

hour of our commute.

—Ahhem

And while you're out there dodging cars, remember every single molecule of living matter has, at one time or another, passed through the asshole of a worm.

CHAPTER 21

Dry Bread Wants a Harley

Dry Bread is fat with cash and is knocking at my door on an early winter morning. During the previous Tour de France, Pen-Pen said he was coming to my house in da Uuu-Esss to buy Le Harley. I said, "Yeah sure, come on over after the season and we'll cruise around on our Harleys." "Yezzzz," said Pen-Pen, "buuuttt I want ze Heritage Zoftail." "Yeah, no problem, come on over; we'll buy a Harley and cruise around the Southwest." I knew he would never show up, 'cause every single guy in the peloton told me they were going to do the same thing and never showed.

So it came as somewhat of a surprise when Ronan Pensec and his wife showed up on my doorstep in Santa Fe, New Mexico. "Pen-Pen," I say, "how the hell are ya?" Ronan says, "I have come for ze Harley."

"All right, yeah, no problem, come on in." Ronan then hands me a thick wad of cash. "I want ze Harley," he says, "and 500 kilos of ze acids amino." "Uh, sure, no problem."

So we load into my truck and drive down to Albuquerque to the Harley dealership, where it just so happens they have a beautiful, brand new Heritage Softail, all black and chrome, for $19,500. "We'll take that one."

Dry Bread Wants a Harley

"Oh, really?" says the salesman. "How will you be paying for that?" "Um, cash," I say. When you wear the Tour de France yellow jersey like Pen-Pen did for a few days, and then your teammate wins the race, especially if your teammate is caped in class like LeMonster, you become fat with ze cash.

So we bought helmets for Pen-Pen and his femme, leather chaps, biker boots, jeans, leather jackets, electric vests, windshield saddle bags, straight pipes, and finally, without which Ronan wouldn't proceed, a pair of whitewall tires. Pen gave me a "g" for helping him out, and the dealership loved me like a brother.

But Pensec had never ridden a motorcycle before. And the next part of his plan was to ride with femme all over the Southwest. So I had to show him how to shift, how to brake, how to start the dang thing. Pen-Pen kept getting the brake and clutch mixed up and nearly crashed us about twenty times as we crawled hurky-jerky back to Santa Fe, while Chiara and his wife drove a truckload of aminos back to the house.

Then the Pen-Pens loaded up and split for Navajo parts unknown.

Chiara and I sat in pure wonder, watching the family Pensec chug off into the distance on top of thirty-grand worth of American Dream.

"Shit," I said and spit in the red dirt. "How do ya like that? We chucked steel like slaves to help Hamstring win the Giro, and we sure as shit ain't laundering cash in some exotic foreign locale like king of the dang planet." As a matter of fact, I was on probably the only team in the history of cycling whose leader kept his prize split after winning a major Tour.

Three weeks later, Dry Bread is back. They have been baked bright red by the wind and sun and have a 2-inch-thick crust of splattered insects stuck to them. They show us some pictures Ronan took of all the hot spots—like Monument Valley, Grand Canyon, Vegas, et cetera, et cetera . . . plus la femme having her hair combed and braided by an old Navajo woman inside a very cool hogan, and Ronan doggin' down on fry bread and mutton stew. Pen calls a friend who works at Air France and gets the bike shipped back to France, loaded with 1,000 kilos of amino.

"Shit," I said and spit in the dirt as the Pensecs left. "How do ya like that? I can't even get a job and that frog wanker is king of the bloody planet."

Remember: "Don't trust blind beggars who walk without canes."

CHARACTERS

Pen–Pen, Dry Bread = Ronan Pensec

LeMonster = Greg LeMond

Hamstring = Andy Hampsten

CHAPTER 22

Lance and the
Dipped in
Ding-dong Doodle
Down in Dixie

When Bob Roll got a call from Lance Armstrong in early April 1998, the stage was set for an epic training trip to the backwoods of North Carolina. This is Bobke's diary:

April 10

"Whoa," I said as I put down the phone. "That was Lance Armstrong," I added in amazement. "What did he want?" my wife asked. "He wants me to go to Boone, North Carolina, for a ten-day training camp with him and Chris Carmichael." "Well, what did you tell him?" asked *mein vrouw.* "Hell yes!" I yelled.

It seems that Lance would like a training partner during a build-up period, as we approach the height of the cycling calendar. I am at a point in my year where I've finished the early-season stage races and need to fine-tune my fitness before the NORBA series begins at Big Bear, California (May 16–17). Big Bear is a savage test of climbing ability and technical endurance. Most often, a wispy super-climber with excellent descending skills is the only type of pro capable of winning this absurd death march. I think the race promoters (Fat Wallet and Bomb Spygold) should just check your weight when you sign on, and give the prizes according to how close to 95 pounds you can get yourself. If there was a boxing round-robin for time bonuses beforehand, you would see an entirely different podium at the end. Halfway through this horror show, hike-a-biking up some preposterous fall line, half an hour behind the lobster boys, I would dearly love to get Gouldy, Tink, Cadel, Nedly, et al. in the ring for three rounds. But since that's not likely to happen in this lifetime, I'll have to resolve myself to hard training, long intervals, and no bacon. I hope this training camp with Lance will be a step in the right direction.

April 16

Good Lord, where in the hell is Boone, North Carolina? It sure as hooch ain't near any airports. It sure as pooch ain't near Antioch or Mount Zion, Moab or Gideon, but is as close to heaven as any town can be (at least according to the local banjo-playin' moonshiners). Da Da Ding Ding Ding Ding Ding Da Da Ding Ding Daaooong Da Da Da Dong Ding Ding Da Ring Ding.

"Are you sure about this place, Kid?" I ask Chris as we drive through pea-soup-thick fog. "Nope," the Kid says, slightly alarmed. "I mean, hasn't Lance seen 'Easy Rider' or 'Deliverance' on The Late Show?" I say to Chris. "I mean, I like you guys all right—L-I-K-E, like okay? Don't force me to love you guys." Me and the Kid drivin' like banshees in the pure boondocks can't stop laughin' time enough to cry.

Bob Roll: Lance, how did you find this place?
Lance Armstrong: We raced through these hills during the Tour DuPont.
BR: How did you find this cabin at the top of this hollow?
LA: Through the Internet.

Lance and the Dipped in Ding–dong Doodle Down in Dixie

BR: Under what? Dentistry Anonymous?

LA: Laugh now, you freaks, but tomorrow we're doing ergometer tests.

April 17

Appalachian State University (In)Human(e) Performance Lab: Chris has reasoned that doing some tests before, and again after, his camp would give us a pretty accurate idea of the training we'll need for the rest of the year. I'll buy that, but how 'bout we test at half effort and multiply by two? "No," says the Kid. "Just askin'," says I.

I was first up on the ergometer. Everything was going along pretty smooth (during the warm-up), until the actual test began and the resistance was factored in. I'm sweatin' away, sufferin' like a dog, but that isn't enough; they have to skewer my finger and start draining blood every two minutes. Now I'm pouring sweat, suffering, and bleeding like a pig—the only finish line, your heart detonating.

The 1990s are tough on a biker, sheezus. Then they try to drown your sorry rat ass for the

☆ ☆ ☆

Lance's test seemed to go a lot smoother, way less skewering from Nosferatu's children, and no bottom-of-a-deep well histrionics in the fat tank.

submersion test. Cormac McCarthy takin' notes in the corner with Erskine Caldwell, just so they can tell you what you already know: You're a fat puke who will never look like Miguel Martinez. Lance's test seemed to go a lot smoother, way less skewering from Nosferatu's children, and no bottom-of-a-deep-well histrionics in the fat tank.

We then went to the local Boone bike shop to get some supplies and maps of the area. While they worked on Lance's well-worn big chainring, I whipped out a BMX bike from the display floor and tried the first BMX freestyle trick of my life—a back wheel stoppie hopping in place. That tam-o'-shanter jack-knifed out from under me, bounced off Lance's forearm and krieged into the display case, sending me ass-over-nipples to the rice-paper-thin carpet over concrete floor. "Dang!" I jumped up cursin'— "You saw me, Kid. I almost had it there."

Boone, North Carolina, is hilly. Watauga County hasn't got a flat or tailwind road in it. Our afternoon ride took us around Beech Mountain of Tour DuPont fame. On the backside, we saw an honest-to-God, deep-Southern-fried, 100-percent authentic, mountain gnome, psycho-billy freak. I thought documentary subjects like himself were only on PBS or a figment of James Dickey's imagination. He called out from his tore-up porch as we climbed by: "Revenuers and Padyrollers, git yerself someways else."

"Did you see that, Lance?" I asked, to make sure I wasn't conjuring an image from my almost completely desiccated dub.-T vapor-consciousness. "I'm sure I did" said Lance, easing my mind a bit. Anyway, it was a great ride through gorgeous country.

BR: How did you feel about today's testing?
LA: They have a really good lab, which surprised me a bit, but the numbers from the test were pretty much where we thought I would be. Maybe even a little better. Since I've had this head cold lingering from before I came out here, I thought the numbers would have been worse. I do have to get a couple of kilos off, though. Next Friday's tests will be a lot better, I hope.

April 18

Lord have mercy. Today was an epic like I haven't ridden in years. Last night, Chris suggested we do a 6-hour ride in the hills. At the time, feeling rested and pleasantly plump, I said, "Yeah, that would be great." But this morning, with rain pissing down like all over the world, I thought we might do 3 or even 2 hours. "No way, baby," said Lance. "It is on for a full 6."

Not an hour into the ride, still on the "main" highway, we are already lost. Not that our map is that bad, but these must be the worst-charted hills in the country. From there, we turned off into the backwoods and deep hollows of Eastern Tennessee and North Carolina. Here is where the pavement ends and the locals have no use whatsoever for street signs. We stopped at nearly every intersection and literally had to forage through the underbrush to find street signs. Every place we stopped, not a single person ever came out of their houses to wonder what two skinny-puppy, soakin' wet, obviously lost cyclists who might need directions were doing up their way.

After 3 hours on dirt and four flat tires, we finally hit pavement again. Tarmac never felt so smooth. We stopped for food, just as I was about to bonk. Two sips of spicy V-8 and one Oreo cookie and Lance was ready to leave. He ate his food bar before the clerk even rang him up. That wasn't like the 7-Eleven team food stops, I guarantee you. We used to have full five-course sit-down drag-out picnics, complete with live entertainment (me or Link usually, jiggin', singing German sailor tunes, or the occasional operatic flight of fancy Donizetti, please). But away we went, floggin' away at ourselves until 5 hours, 58 minutes had gone by (a 2-minute rain concession. Whoopee!).

Ahhhh, a nice hot shower, hearty lunch, and a solid nap will set me to rights, I said, as we got home. No dice—laundry, clean and repair bikes, get groceries, and no lunch for you, fat lazy slob. Dang, you young lions are going to be the death of this old war-horse.

BR: How did you like them apples, Lance?

LA: That was a killer ride—all those dirt roads, hilly and rain all day. I was kinda surprised how good I felt, all in all, but 6 hours in the rain with unpaved hills is still hard. Plus our map sucks.

April 19

Oh my word, now the sky is crying. Pouring, under-a-shower rain every single moment of a 4-hour jaunt. The camp has now begun to take on its defining characteristics: (1) Rain; (2) Hills; (3) Rain and Hills; (4) Laughter. Me and Lance have been laughing non-stop about all the kooks who race bikes—ourselves included. Noah would have looked up to these heavens, grinned, and fetched his hammer. Today, my legs felt like solid turds from a toxic waste dump.

BR: Was today miserable or what?

LA: Booby, I was soaked 5 minutes out the door.

BR: My legs seized with waterlogging 10 minutes later.

LA: I felt pretty good, actually. Ridin' in that is why Belgians and Dutchies can race so well in it. I can see how they would get used to it with day-in, day-out training. Racing would just become second nature. Still, I'd rather see the sun at least once while we're here.

April 20

Shagged 'til fragged, tagged, and bagged. Seven hours with no stops, windy, endless hills, Nascar wannabes . . . but thankfully, no rain. Just sweet sunshine for a real-deal, world-class training ride. We climbed for the first hour, then literally went under the Blue Ridge Parkway, then a long descent took us into Burke County, and after 5.5 hours, a huge climb took us back up to regain our altitude. This has been a side-by-side ride, until the long climb. Then and there, Lance began to turn the screws. O-U-C-H, ouch! I tried to keep a bit of fuel in my reserve tank, but that wick was burnt to the nub by the time we topped out. Lance was going well and I was, well, I was going.

I can't believe how good the ridin' is out here, and in all my years I have never heard about it. Right after the ride, I mean direct, junge, Lance was on his computer. He was checking stock-market prices, sending and receiving e-mails, downloading his heart-rate monitor . . . tappin' on the keys with big morale fervor like a true new-centurion. I was pure old school—feet up in bed, listening to Gaelic folk songs about the potato famine. The images floating up before me were of the sunken eyes and bloated bellies that compelled Irish people to emigrate from the Old Country to places like Boone. And here I am, still ridin', still Irish, and still hungry.

BR: Gawd, how majestic was today's ride?

LA: Don't even try to tell me. I can't remember ever doing a 200-plus-K, 7-plus-hour training ride like this. Two up like that in these hills is more like a 260-kilometer race. If this doesn't get me back on track, I don't know what will.

☆　☆　☆

> I was pure old school—feet up in bed, listening to Gaelic folk songs about the potato famine. The images floating up before me were of the sunken eyes and bloated bellies that compelled Irish people to emigrate from the Old Country to places like Boone.

April 21

Double Pack Restack Back on the Rack. That is, two rides today, back to back with just enough time in between to get totally locked up. On many of the old-time shacks around here, they used rough-hewn planks for the side boards that are planed once, direct from the tree trunk; and on the first ride, my legs were as stiff as these hardwoods. I am beat down and stood up like I haven't been since the 1980s. Great gosh a'mighty, it feels like a long time since I was Lance's age—with nothing but power reserves, endless morale, and a horribly unslaked thirst to obliterate all Philistines, freaks, punks, naysayers, and doomsdayers.

Amazingly, the second ride went a bit better and my legs had some spring to them. This morning, the Kid said that two rides today would actually speed recovery. I thought to myself, "No bloody way." But after doing both rides, I'll be dipped in wong-dong doodle; the Kid was right on. I had forgotten just how hard it is to train at the highest level of this sport. I am being reminded day by day, climb by climb, hour after long hour, and I thank God my training has gone pretty well so far this year, or I would be pushin' up mountain laurel right here in the great Appalachian Mountains.

BR: What do you think about that—two rides the day after an epic 7-hour ride?

LA: It isn't pretty, that is for sure. My legs were feeling it today, boy. But this training is going so well, I might get on the phone and see about riding in Atlanta this weekend. How sweet will it be when I post up again? I feel like winning is a possibility in the not-too-distant future.

April 22

Oh Lord, can't ya hear me cry? Another savage epic. High of 40 degrees, pissin' ass, shag-nasty rain, just carvin' the flab off me like a molten razor blade through room-temperature butter. There is no rest for the wicked, and no ticket to ride. Just ceaseless coos of madness from the slightly round gyroscope in my innermost brain that slings me forward. The highway never ends, but this 6-hour hit parade did—right at the top of Beech Mountain. The name says it all. Lance fragged me miles from the top, and

Lance and the Dipped in Ding–dong Doodle Down in Dixie

I was left crawling like a salamander in my 21-cog, blowing chunks of lung. Like I said, I be fit or I be dead. After sixteen climbs today, no stops at all, no stories of the old days, just side-by-side hard drivin', I am totally wasted.

BR: Lance, is it something I said, and you guys don't like me and you're trying to kill me?

LA: Who's trying to kill whom, Booby? I don't believe I've done a week of training as concentrated as this in weather that is so awful.

BR: I can't believe it can rain this much outside of Belgium.

LA: We've been truly hosed with the weather. But when the sun finally does come out we are going to fly.

April 23

This hurtin' kind of got a hold on this sweet child, but a 2-hour recovery ride for a heaven-sent rest day will keep me keepin' on. Superman is strong, Batman is righteous with quwan toys,

☆ ☆ ☆

Superman is strong, Batman is righteous with quwan toys, and Spiderman can stick to walls like some wrath-filled voyeur, but 200-proof ratboy sticks to the cellars and sewers . . .

and Spiderman can stick to walls like some wrath-filled voyeur, but 200-proof ratboy sticks to the cellars and sewers—seething and riotous—planning cold revenge with a survival edict passed undiluted to the here and now from the spark of creation, venomous and coiled beyond vexation from Liggett junkies, pitiful ghouls, and sissified fools.

Lance and I were floatin' down the runway, tapped into centuries-old conflicts between man, state, and nature. Refugees from the hillbilly feudal wards pointing bony fingers, until confronted with ice-cold death stares auguring out of our pale blue eyes.

I can't hardly believe the end of this camp is nigh and tomorrow we will be back to the lab and then to Charlotte to fly home.

BR: Boy, I'm about to crack. I needed that ride today to recover some.

LA: Yeah, last night I was pretty tired, but I feel great this evening. I can't wait to tear up those tests tomorrow.

BR: Do you think that the numbers will be off, since we trained so hard this week?

LA: No way. You will be surprised to see how much we've improved over the first test. As a matter of fact, I'm puttin' $25 of Chris's cash for the first guy to get up to 600 watts.

CC: Not my cash, but I'll pay you a dollar for every watt over 550 that you get to.

LA: That's a bet!

April 24

Back to Appalachian State and into the lab. Whoa—I guess the word is out that Lance is in the house. Our little three-man training camp and lab test with the Doc and a few interns has turned into a full-blown media hootenanny. Lance's recent cancer fight, plus his incredible victories on these roads just before, have compelled all the local paparazzi, news crews from Charlotte, much of the faculty, and about half of the student body to be crammed into the lab. Lance took it all in stride, but I got claustrophobic all of a sudden. I turned straight into DeNiro's Travis Bickell trying to liberate Iris, a.k.a. Easy, in "Taxi Driver": "You talkin' to me?"

This time, Lance went first on the ergometer. The Doc and his crew were very professional, and primed for Lance to rip it up. Lance didn't disappoint. As a matter of fact, he tore their machines up! Lance reached the limit of their ergometer with plenty of power to spare. After 25 minutes at over 500 watts, Lance had to step off, 'cause smoke was billowing up from the cranks as the rack of torture fried. The Doc was amazed. "We're going to have to recalibrate this data," was his conclusion.

In the meantime, your ever-lovin' Uncle Blobkey was doin' my best not to drown in the fat tank. I put my head down, exhaled, and proceeded to sink down like a rebar-crisscrossed slab of concrete. The Doc was psyched with my skin-fold test—4 percent upper thigh, 3-plus inner tricep, etc., etc . . . until he got to my back. "Gee, your back is still quite thick," he said. "And I don't believe I've ever seen hair quite so thick on someone's back." Oh, I'm savin' that for my bald spot when I move to Hollywood for my next gig as the Baywatch dude.

Lance's improvement after just one week of training was astounding. There's a twister comin', brewing up from deep in the heart of Texas, advising all freaky-deaky, kookie-pukie, dipped-in-dung road hogs to tighten down your ratchet buckles. What the human body is capable of cannot be theorized in textbooks and lab data. Consequently, no training program should be without savage radical efforts undertaken with extreme duress. Lance is living proof.

Time had come to leave Boone, and Lance launched our rental mini-van out of town like Jeff Gordon off the line at Talledega. What else to do in Charlotte except drink espresso with Sandy and Georgio at Gita, and stay at George Hincapie's lush pad?

BR: Any good impressions about the training camp, the weather not withstanding?

LA: Well, the testing showed a huge improvement, but not really more than I expected. I probably lost as much body fat from laughing as the riding. The laughter definitely died off towards the end of camp, though.

BR: Yeah, I got kinda grim after old Noah went floating by.

LA: But all in all, it was a good camp. We just need a better deal from the weather next time. What are you doing the first weekend in June?

BR: Comin' back to Boone?

LA: That's right, Rollercoaster.

CHAPTER 23

Nine Guesses

Armstrong was begat by Indurain, Indurain was begat by LeMond, LeMond was begat by Hinault, Hinault was begat by Merckx, Merckx was begat by Anquetil, Anquetil was begat by Coppi. . . . But Coppi sprang up from the barren waste made fertile by the blood of a beautiful people of a war-ravaged country. God wasn't available.

The spring classics were written on Dante's parchment—right where "The Divine Comedy" disintegrates into the "Inferno."

The Eurodogs call LeMond (pronounced "lemon" by the French) Jack, after the actor Jack Lemmon. Jack can do whatever he wants—when or wherever. He is Jack.

Every time you are caught behind or in a huge fifty-man pileup, there is a strange, putrid, but very particular odor. It took me years to figure it out. It is the smell of burning flesh being peeled off the world's fittest men as they slide across the asphalt.

Flanders is the worldwide capital of bicycle racing. Any 7-year-old Flemish schoolchild knows 100 times more about cycling than all Americans combined.

Watch every movie ever made about the Mafia. Then watch "La Strada," by Fellini. Then drink eight espressos and a bottle of Chianti. Then flagellate in front of a Sophia Loren poster for six days and nights. Now you are ready to be crucified by the Giro.

Watch every movie ever made about Vietnam. Then watch "Auvoir Les Enfants," by Truffualt. Then shoot Novocain into your brain and drink a bottle of champagne. Then burn your fingernails off with a Bic lighter. Then kill your cat with a shovel. Now you are ready to be buried alive by Le Tour.

You can stand up all you want. You can eat all the ice cream you want. Just don't let Eddy Merckx catch you doing either.

As a pro cyclist, your fame and fortune are soon forgotten, but your suffering as a racer stays with you as long as you live.

CHAPTER 24

A Day at the Fair

Before the Berlin wall came down, before the disintegration of the Soviet bloc, before Gontchar, Konyshev, Berzin, or Ekimov, there was Lada. Even before the Russian superteam Alfa Lum, there was Team Lada: the worst team in the history of cycling.

The sponsorship of the team consisted of one used Lada sedan—period. The team consisted of four Russians nobody had ever heard of and one director (who also was soigneur, mechanic, driver, manager, cook, doctor, and coach). The team rode on ancient Colnagos from the USSR amateur team's throw-away stock. The components were an amazing mix of brands, parts, years, and gear ratios. The uniforms were a gulagesque mix of new and old Lycra and wool, semi-faded to downright ragged. The crash-damage repair to shorts and jerseys was a crazy patchwork of stitches to patches to—I swear to God—tape. Complaining about your own bike or uniform seemed pretty silly, compared to what the Lada guys put up with.

They mainly raced the *kermesse* circuit of Belgium and the Netherlands (kermesse is Dutch for "a fair") but occasionally popped up at smaller stage races in Spain, Germany, and Italy. They survived off the pittance of start money a pro receives just for entering. Between races, I can only imagine how they got by. They were the standing joke of the entire peloton: "Watch what you say or you'll end up on Lada," or "My bike (legs, head, morale . . .) went Lada on me (fell apart completely)," or "I've had as many massages as a Lada guy this month (none)" . . . on and on until the very word "Lada" took on an almost mythical, absolute rock-bottom meaning.

It would be cool to report that these guys developed into competent pros and a couple got jobs on some of the bigger pro teams. But this being the savage garden of pro cycling and not some Hollywood scriptwriter's imagination, that is not exactly what happened. In fact, those four Russians rode as poorly as they looked. They were without doubt the most pitiful wankers to ever sign on. At the slightest hint of acceleration, all four went straight out the back—and there they stayed for the duration, doing a four-man team time trial at 32.8 kph.

Their raggedy-man-on-a-bike approach set them apart—but they were defined by their unwavering support of each other: They always rode only as slow as their slowest guy. Year upon year and month after month, rain, sun, wind, Belgium, Holland, Germany, or Spain, from February through October, they employed the exact same modus operandi: The peloton would speed up, and they'd get dropped immediately, never to be seen again. If you were ever dropped all the way back to the Lada boys, you knew you must have a lethal dose and had better drop out—D-I-R-E-C-T. Their amazing tenacity in the face of such embarrassing incompetence was hard to believe. But even more amazing still was how Team Lada rode in Knokke-Heist, a Belgian coastal town, in 1991.

We were in Knokke-Heist on May 30 for the town's annual kermesse, which had actually become more of a semi-classic due to length (200 km), time of year (before the Tour), quality of racers (every top team from

A Day at the Fair

Belgium, the Netherlands, France, and even Italy and Spain), and the fact that the race now was eligible for UCI points. The wind was blowing hard off the coast only a couple of blocks away from the start line, and the race was bound to be very hard from the start.

At the same time, my morale was as low as "Paeche de doed" (the guy from Flemish lore who welcomed you to hell). I had been living and racing in Europe for a long time and had been witness to many discouraging things. Plus, during the transition from Team 7-Eleven to Motorola, to my complete dismay, I was left off the roster. I was also utterly shattered from the previous Tour de France, and when I finally got the call up just before the Motorola team presentation in mid-January, I hadn't done nearly enough training over the winter. That spring, no matter how many miles I put in, my legs hadn't felt good the whole season—at a time when I was usually among the best and at my personal best. I couldn't help but reflect on these things as we drove in the team Benzes from Kortrijk to Knokke-Heist. By the time we got there, I was totally bummed.

The sign-on was in a typical, smoky Belgian café. Ahhh . . . the smell of beer, cigars, and wasted-by-noon Oost-Vlanderen bike kooks, who hadn't bathed since Freddy Maertens ruled these streets. As I walked back to the team car after signing on, I passed by the omnipresent frite stand. The frites (double the fat in an American french fry, then drown it in mayonnaise) smelled great, as the sage words of cycling prophet Luc "the drifter" Eysermans came to me: "Never, ever, never eat frites." I vowed not only to eat frites, but blood sausage as well (the lowest point for any racer's morale). That's when I saw them. . . .

Team Lada pulled up to the square in the Lada team car. The car spewed smoke and coughed and wheezed to a stop, and the solemn Russians filed out. They were as bedraggled as ever. But as they looked out across the square and saw the team buses and cars of Panasonic, Buckler,

Hitachi, PDM, Z, Carrera, Motorola, Lotto, and ONCE . . . their normal look of resignation took on an added element of alarm.

"Horrorshow Bezoomy!" I called out to them, borrowing from "Clockwork Orange." As usual, when I said that, they looked at me as if I'd just touched down from a Mir mission to Mars. I don't know why, but seeing the Lada boys gave my morale a little boost. Not great heaps of ready-to-fly morale, but enough to figure out a way to enjoy myself a bit. So I decided to attack like a psycho right at the start and see if they would let me go for the first time in my career. And that is just what I did.

I hit the start runnin' and had half a minute by the first corner, only a few hundred meters after the start. I banked hard into the turn, felt the silk sew-ups grip tight, and just as I stood on the pedals to accelerate out of the turn, my front tire rolled off the rim. My graceful arc morphed into a spastic weave, boring straight for the crowd. In any other country on earth, I would have had a nice, soft landing into some unsuspecting spectator. But not Flanders. Those crafty Vlaamse bike fans jumped out of my way and I krieged rim-first into the curb. Pow! Over the bars, I went flying and landed on my ass, holdin' my ankles. The crowd gathered around me, as I sat there shakin' my head, and just stared in wonder that I hadn't been hurt or even lost any skin. Soothing to my ego, though, the peloton did not see me laid out in the first turn or even up the road. The boys thought I had really taken off, and the whole peloton began to chase hard. By the time I got up to change my wheel, the Lada team was already dropped.

Vroom-vroom-vroom, car after car went by. "Bloody, f—ing hell, where in rat-puke fudge is our car?" Finally, the broom wagon went by, but no Motorola team car. It seems the Belgian federation had just enacted a new rule that anyone in a team car following a pro race had to be an accredited mechanic, director, soigneur, or doctor. A racer's girl-friend from the States didn't count. So I sat there, out of sight around the

A Day at the Fair

corner, not more than 50 yards from our team car, as a commissaire tried to extract one of my teammates' girlfriends from our car, nobody understanding anyone.

It finally dawned on me to walk backward along the course to find the turd-pile team car and change my own dang wheel. And there it was, surrounded by a crowd of frantic Vlaamsemen screaming that I needed a wheel, and an equally frantic Belgian commissaire trying to drag a petrified chick-a-chick-a-boom-boom out of our car. At last, Doug—the prince of Scottsdale—Ritter saw me running toward him wheel (without tire) aloft, screaming obscenities. I changed my wheel and began to chase flat out. I was already 5 minutes down after only 10 kilometers. The Russians, though, had lost 3 minutes.

I kept my head down, blastin' across the bedrock, trying to get back to the peloton. I almost crashed into the Lada team car, as it followed the grim Russians in the midst of yet another futile team time trial. After another 30-kilometer solo, I caught the caravan and took another 10 kilometers to get back in the bunch. I was quite pleased to regain contact, and I was determined not to get dropped—even though the next 100 kilometers were really fast, with constant attacks going up the road.

Finally, the right combination of guys from the right teams got away, and the peloton sat up. In the break were Frans Maassen from Buckler and Marc Sergeant from Panasonic. They worked perfectly together and quickly gained 3 minutes. The two strongest teams with their best riders were well established and flying up the road.

The mood in the peloton, having conceded the win, turned suddenly amicable. The wind stopped, the sun was out, the boys had been racing flat out all day, and the best guys were in the break. All that remained was a nice, easy promenade to the finish. Thirty kilometers from the finish, Maassen and Sergeant already had a 7-minute lead. With 15 kilometers to go, they had almost 10 minutes. The Russians, meanwhile, were only 5 minutes behind the absolutely creeping peloton. And with one lap to go, the Russians caught the peloton.

Whoa!!! The whole group cheered in disbelief as they saw the four Russians—for the first time ever—in the main group at the end of a race. The pack kind of ambled along in a general state of merriment, without any idea or care of what was going on in the break, now only 4 minutes up the road. As the finish got closer, the usual increase of tempo in the pack began to take shape. Not as intense as if the pack were racing to win, but pretty fast, nonetheless. The Russians tried to keep Romanov, their fastest sprinter, near the front and out of the wind, as even 3rd in a big kermesse would be a miraculous result for them. What no one in the pack knew was that the break had ceased to work and was coming back like a stone.

Both Frans and Marc have a pretty wicked spurt. Neither was willing to do one iota more work than the other. At the same time, both were trying to sit on without working. As the kilometers clicked down to the finish, so did their advantage.

Still, with 5 kilometers to go, the break held a 2-minute lead. By now, the peloton was charging full-blown and thundering toward the line. Maassen and Sergeant had come to an absolute crawl. Side-by-side, slower and slower, they rode staring at each other—neither willing to give even a centimeter away.

When we caught Maassen and Sergeant with about 3 kilometers to go, utter chaos ensued. Every guy realized he had a chance to win, and everyone attacked simultaneously. Louis De Koning of Panasonic launched the hardest; he was joined by Marek Kulas, a Pole on the Belgian team, La William, and they both put their heads down and belted for the finish. Maybe they didn't see Ivan Romanov on their wheel, but more likely, they were convinced that nobody on Team Lada could be capable of any kind of sprint spud whatsoever. They were wrong. Romanov unleashed a furious and powerful sprint in the final 100 meters. Kulas was instantly vanquished, and Romanov had just enough gas to get around De Koning and hit the finish line arms aloft as he let out a holler of pure wonder and joy. Even the most jaded and wasted Eurodog couldn't help but smile.

At that point in my career, I was just about ready to pack my bags and scoot home. I had seen so much corruption, while literally riding myself into the ground, that both my mind and body were at the limit of my capacities. But seeing Ivan Romanov of Team Lada win that race so amazed me, I was able to renew my resolve and understand that just about anything can happen—and usually does—when you're racing Belgian kermesses. I realized that if you are in the race, you have a chance. If you stick by your team through thick and thin, you increase your chance. And if you allow what rends your body and striates your mind to nourish your spirit, you cannot lose. . . .

After getting cleaned up and loaded into the team cars, I realized I had completely forgotten about those frites.

CHAPTER 25

The Night before Amstel

T'was the night before Amstel and all through the chateau

Not a pharmacist was stirring, not even on tiptoe.

The I.V.s were hung from the chandelier with care,

In hopes that the team doctor soon would be there.

The bikers, feet up, were resting in bed,

While visions of podiums danced in their heads.

And the mechanics in apron, and directeur in cap

Had just settled down for a nice pre-race nap.

When out in the car park, there arose such a clatter,

I sprang from the hammock to see what was the matter.

Away to the window, I lurched like a drunk,

And saw our team van being robbed by some punk.

The streetlight on the pavement and pissing-down rain

Gave the luster of suffering to Amstel's pain.

The Night before Amstel

When, what to my seen-it-all eyes should appear,
But a UCI dope doc and nine tiny samples of fear.

With a little phlebotomist so shaky and slow,
I knew in a moment my blood would soon flow.
More rapid than a hamster, my heart did beat.
"Yes, doc, it's 3 hours since I had something to eat."

Now, Virenque! Now, Brochard!
Now, Zülle and Dufaux!
Now, Massi! Now, Chiappa!
Now, Planckaert and Moreau!

To the top of the podium, their hands against the wall.
To the dismay of all children, though some deny all.
So to the top of the forearm, the blood cops they drew,
With a sleigh-full of syringes—and Hein Verbruggen, too.

And then in a twinkling, I heard on my telly,
The whinge-ing and moaning of old, sad, fat Willy.
Yes, it was true, that Voet had been caught.
And now, it was certain, Festina was hot.

Dressed all in s—t, from his head to his foot,
With both lies and truth, Roussel's good name was soot.
A bundle of drugs, Voet had flung in his trunk,
Are these racers full of talent, or pharmaceutical junk?
Their eyes—how they twinkled! Their actions so quick.
Their corneas so white . . . because their blood was so thick.

CHAPTER 26

Into the Twenty-first Century

Here are Bob Roll's fearless predictions for what might happen in cycling—and other realms—in the upcoming century.

In the year 2000, Lance will win the Tour de France by the largest margin since World War II. Stuart O'Grady will slip away from the field in the Olympic road race into the final breakaway containing Michele Bartoli of Italy, Marc Wauters of Belgium, Dmitri Konyshev of Russia, and Andreï Tchmil, also of Belgium. Konyshev and Tchmil will chase each other down, Wauters will chase Bartoli for Tchmil, and O'Grady will win the sprint for gold. Australia will go wild with cycling mania as O'Grady is the only gold to go to the host country. (Cadel Evans takes the cross-country silver after an early flat and a heroic chase that falls a knobby-width short of a flying Frischy—finally winning the title that bad luck has prevented for so long.)

In 2001, Outdoor Life Network will lavishly present the Tour with 2 hours of live racing every day. Lance will win for the third time by the smallest margin ever: 5 seconds over Jan Ullrich. Lance will announce his retirement from the podium to form a rock band called Torchrow, with Michael Ward (formerly of the Wallflowers) on guitar, Chris Novoselic (formerly of Nirvana) on bass, Madonna on tambourine, Ruthie Matthes on vocals, and Lance on drums. A fifty-city tour will commence in Austin on August 1 from the back of a 1961 Caddy Fleetwood limo driven by me. The roadies will all be former U.S. Postal roadies.

In 2004, Tinker Juarez will be the last sponsored mountain bike pro in the world, riding for Tomac Bikes, which has replaced Giant (JT's fat-tire sponsor) as the world's largest maker of XC bikes. Chinese mountain bikers will sweep the Athens Olympics but fail the drug tests. The gold medal will be won by Matt Kelly who is the highest placed all-natural athlete in the race. He finishes 47th. Juli Furtado comes out of retirement and obliterates the women's field riding a prototype single-speed hybrid track-recumbent bike with Shimano components made from a new alloy of hemp and glitter.

In 2007, gasoline will cost $93.47 per gallon. Bill Gates is the last person to own a car on earth. Everyone else rides bikes and pelts Gates's car with poopy diapers as he drives by. Ruthie Matthes quits Torchrow to make her cycling comeback and is replaced by Ruby Roll. Steve Larsen—who was cryogenically frozen in 1997—thaws out, does a hostile takeover of NORBA, replacing Phil Milburn, who is charged with selling bootleg Snoop Doggy Dog CDs and Ohio Players eight-track tapes from his B.O.B trailer.

In 2010, Energizer replaces the bunny with Ned Overend after Nedly wins his twelfth XTERRA final.

Into the Twenty-first Century

In 2011, Marco Pantani is arrested while lying on the private resort beach of Cesenatico for not paying to rent the required umbrella. Unable to pay his fine, he spends one week in jail and does forty hours of community service paving the bike path along the beach. Kevin Livingston retires from his job as roadie for Torchrow and is elected governor of Texas. Shawn Palmer is elected president of the United States in a heated battle with Jesse Ventura. Napalm body-slams the aging wrestler into the turn buckle to break the tie. Bobby Julich finally has a crash-free Tour de France to take the yellow jersey from Alex Zülle, who crashes into the Arc de Triomphe on the last day of the Tour. NFL and NHL cancel their seasons because nobody will carry their 10 tons of gear on a bicycle.

In 2018, Geoff LeMond wins his fourth Tour de France, breaking the American record for Tour wins, set by Greg in 1990 and tied by Lance in 2001. Bob Roll is finally recognized as a great linguist for coining the word "sassified"—to be pacified through satisfaction.

In 2024, Luke Armstrong wins his first Tour de France and vows to demolish all his dad's records. The western United States returns to its naturally rural population density as people realize that riding 40 miles across the desert to buy a doughnut and some nail polish under your own power is way too difficult. Gigantic ghost towns spring up in Durango, Scottsdale, El Paso, and Palm Springs.

In 2025, Andy Hampsten emerges from his self-imposed exile in Toscana to lead a team of U.S. juniors in a tour of all the eastern European stage races for under-23 riders. During the Tour of Uzbekistan, Andy has a series of graphic flashbacks to his own days as a junior under Eddie B. and convinces all the riders to join a circus headed for Mongolia. Andy returns to the U.S. and moves into Steve Tilford's basement. Tilly and Andy reintroduce Barum sew-ups to a rapt American consumer base. Dave Cullinan quits his job as a Las Vegas Elvis impersonator to join Brian Lopes, Mike King, Eric Carter, Shawn Palmer, and Miles Rockwell as male escorts for Princess Sailboat Lines. They ask Johnny T. to join, but since there is no more global warming, his once-arid 1,000 acres is now a thriving mango and guava farm.

In 2028, the Senior Bike Tour is announced with a schedule of races similar to the spring classics, grand tours, and fall world championships. The format is a bit different than pro racing. First of all, the ex-pros are required to take drugs rather than avoid them. Second, bad weather cancels any event, and no hills bigger than an overpass will be climbed. Third, nobody with a current pro license is allowed, which leaves out Ned, Tinker, Bostick, and Wiensey. Amber Ramos wins her fifteenth world XC title after a close battle with Kelsey Phinney—who is looking for new challenges after winning the Tour Féminin, Hewlett-Packard, three Olympic Nordic skiing titles, and annihilating her pops Davis in their bitter Sunday morning Boulder-city-limit-sign sprint rivalry.

In 2029, Frankie Andreu is the president of the United States—his first decree is to print a five-hundred-dollar bill with Dennis Rodman's face. He moves the White House to the County Line Ribshack in Lubbock, Texas, and appoints Joe Parkin as Minister of Propoganda, Zap Espinoza as Minister of Culture, and Luma Randolph as Secretary of the Treasury.

In 2050, Sean Yates finally retires as directeur sportif of the Linda McCartney Cycling Team. He defeats half the pro riders from his team in his send-off race: a 50-mile time trial on the A2 lorry road between London and Ramsgate.

In 2070, the world crude oil reserves finally run out completely. Everything in the world is human- or animal-powered. Pollution is in complete remission and drive-by shootings are a thing of the ancient past.

In 2099, teachers, maids, garbage men, roofers, and bicycle mechanics make more money than venture capitalists, corporate lawyers, real estate speculators, and golf course operators.

CHAPTER 27

51 Things to Do before You Die

Climb Alpe d'Huez the day the Tour de France passes. Watch the entire procession of lunatics. Partake of all alcohol offered to you by the crazed fans on that hill. Cheer like a senseless fanatic for the leaders. Cry like a baby for the sprinters' gruppetto who will be suffering like animals. Take photos—but if you stand in the middle of the road, under no circumstances whatsoever should you knock a racer down.

Own and use regularly any Campy part made before Tullio ascended to heaven on his fiery parallelogram chariot.

Visit Madonna del Ghisallo Chapel and get down on your heathen, Philistine knees and pray. Pray that you don't get obliterated by a car on the narrow roads of Ghisallo.

Own a pair of titanium salt and pepper shakers.

Own a pair of superlight wheels with tubular tires. Curse them like a sailor with Tourette's Syndrome when you have to glue on a new sew-up.

51 Things to Do before You Die

Own a cyclo-cross bike; race it once, and only once.

Ride Kings Ridge to Tin Barn to Skuggs Road. Skinny dip in Lake Sonoma at the end of the ride. Wine taste for the rest of the evening.

Ride across America, stopping in every podunk burg along the way. Rely graciously upon the generosity of strangers. Never ever race across America.

Pick a year, any year, and ride your bike more miles than you drive your car.

Watch Paris-Roubaix from the forest of Wallers.

Ride every cobbled stretch of Paris-Roubaix, but not all at once.

Ride a Ducati motorcycle—the summation of two-wheeled motor-ized nirvana.

Listen to Fausto Coppi sing for a 1950s Italian television show. Hear the angelic, lilting sadness prophesizing his own early death.

Get your photo taken with Eddy Merckx at Interbike, with that glazed look in your star-struck eyes.

Wait in line for a couple of hours at least for Lance's autograph, because those lines are only going to get longer and longer.

Go to a bike camp. Preferably one that is run by a bloated, alcoholic ex-pro.

Volunteer to work at a bike camp for the juniors.

Ride the Blue Ridge Parkway start to finish, north to south. Pull off every chance you get and pass through tiny Smoky Mountain towns like Low Gap, North Carolina; Hillsville, Virginia; Blowing Rock, North Carolina; Ela, North Carolina; and Cokecreek, Tennessee. Don't forget your drawl, y'all. Bring along a book of James Dickey poetry and be sure to rent "Deliverance" at some point.

Watch the Ghent Six-Day while drinking tons of Trappiste beer and smoking about 200 cigarettes. When you're good and fluthered and dizzy from watching the giants of the boards fly around and around, you will begin to see the specters of all the great track racers rising up through the smoke.

The Great North Road, north of London, saw the invention of time trialing. Ride it at 5 o'clock on a Sunday morning.

Climb the Koppenberg in the Flemish Ardennes. Watch the Tour of Flanders pass by and marvel at the speed of leaders like Vandenbroucke, Van Petegem, and Museeuw.

Watch Liège-Bastogne-Liège on the hill at Houffalize. Follow the race for the last 80 kilometers over all the savage climbs like La Redoute, Forges, Sart-Tilman, Sprimont, and Haute Levée.

Sip cappuccino at Bar Volta in Como, Italy, after a huge breakfast of prosciutto, eggs, brioche, and rice.

Get road rash. Do not treat it and let it coagulate into thick strips of leather. Peel them off at a fancy dinner party and chew on them to the absolute horror of the hosts.

51 Things to Do before You Die

Ride the Natchez Trace, preferably with the Lance Armstrong Peloton Project. Do not crash right in front of me, Kevin Livingston, or Dr. Wolf.

Ride in the rain with your cycling buddies covered with European liniment oil, and even though you will still freeze your ass off, you will at least smell like a pro.

Buy a leather hairnet. Only use it while riding on your rollers, or shopping for Mister Sharpies and Krazy Glue.

Ride around Lake Como with a side trip to St. Moritz.

Ride naked at 3 a.m. past your local police station, with a Walkman duct-taped to your left butt cheek, listening to "The Sound of Music."

Ride from San Francisco to Los Angeles along Highway 1 during the gray whale migration.

Watch the U.S. Pro Championship on Manayunk Wall with up to 50,000 like-minded lunatics.

Stitch a St. Christopher medallion to your helmet straps. Don't leave home without it. Reap as you sew.

The Ozarks are calling—ride them.

Count 8 seconds. Imagine, Greg LeMond beat Laurent Fignon by this margin in a race that is 3 weeks long.

Ride your one true love on your handlebars, whispering sweet nothings into your true love's ear.

Learn from Joe Parkin's life story.

Cover your sidewalls with poetry—Blake, Burns, Dylan (Bob or Thomas), Cobain—or your own opus to your semper fi servant, the humble and stoic bicycle.

Be a bike messenger in San Francisco for a month or a decade.

Own a wool jersey.

Do Ragbrai towing a keg of beer in a Burley trailer with a Run-DMC ghetto blaster duct-taped to your handlebars blasting Donna Summer, Bee Gees, Tower of Power, and Harold Melvin and the Blue Notes.

Furrow a deep and long row in loamy, damp singletrack with only God as your witness.

Ride over the Golden Gate Bridge.

Visit the Church of St. John Coltrane in San Francisco.

Ride Slick Rock in Moab, and get fleeced by Rob and Bill at the Rim Supply.

Have dinner with Fred Mengoni in New York City.

Poach Mt. Tam singletrack.

After a long ride in poochy weather, eat blood sausage and frites dipped in mayonnaise, and drink a liter of Trappiste beer.

Look deep into Sean Yates's eyes and say: "You are the greatest of all time."

Memorize ten exclamations from Phil Liggett's Tour coverage. Recite them at the top of your lungs, complete with suave British accent, substituting your buddies' names for the names of the Tour riders at your next group ride.

Call Roland Della Santa at 3:27 a.m. and chant "I am the Walrus" about a hundred times.

Join IMBA. Goo goo ka choo.

CHAPTER 28

Eurotrash and the Texas Tornado

Hey, dream children with your schizoid mazurkas tumbling through your mind. I know how you feel. You dream of pounding across the Pyrénées, with a crazed Eurotrash powerhouse biker's pain account paid in full, and educationally bankrupt and murderous Hessians on your wheel. I know your dreams, but does your VO$_2$max hit the high 80s? Or are your femurs as long as the Golden Gate Bridge? Or are your shoulders narrow and your ass the size of a barn? Or all of the above?

Dream on if not. If so, there is only one more ingredient. Do you enjoy inflicting pain and suffering? Does the thought of heat and freeze-bite, manure in your teeth, and hearing the retarded thousand-year-old dialect of demented nuns fill you with glee?

Remember this: Frat boys your age will be in Florida wasting daddy's trust fund on strippers and beer, while you are suffering like an inquisition hunchback sucking a fat ass for a solid decade. And remember that that decade will not be returned to you when you are 30 and have been cored out like a suckling Christmas pig. Save your rock-star fantasies for vacuous sorority sisters who give a shit. And as high as you climb, you will fall at least as deep.

Eurotrash and the Texas Tornado

So when you see Bobby J. or Johnny V. or Ali D. or Elke B. at VeloSwap, close your whinging hole and whip out your dot-com checkbook and kick down hard for the sacrificial lambs, you heathen frat-freak scum. So what if the gruppetto is littered with *pane e acqua* chumps?

Pray to God you don't fall asleep during a crosswind-battle firefight on Flanders field. I will guarantee you a trip home out of the 'Nam in a short-order-cook body bag. So drink, drink hard, and dream of what might have been.

Lily-livered sun-spotted dowager, ball-breaking neurotic narcissistic hardball Republicans call me all the time and tell me how it is. I don't care. I roll on. Nux vomica love lies bleeding sprout on the Ocaña-Otxoa gravesite as the acquisition-and-merger department coming to a soul kitchen near you misses the point entirely.

People look at me like I'm a natural born mujahedeen when I show up for the club ride with a USPS cap from homedog No. 1 Lancealicious instead of a skid lid, but I roll on. My liver is the size of the Hindenburg; I don't care. People stagger around me as if they are going to live forever, with their SUVs guzzling gas instead of them guzzling booze until they drop.

My idea is this: Pedal your sorry ass up the Ventoux some enchanted July and drink with the Basques 'til you puke. Then drop-kick your Giro and strip naked so you get a sunburn on your bollocks and ride down, weaving between blotto tifosi, screaming Yankee Doodle Dandy at the top of your lungs, 'cause after an epic battle of mythological proportions between Lance, Jan, and Levi, the yellow jersey has finally been painted how it belongs: red, white, and blue. If you live forever, you may see such a thing again, but probably not.

So call the "grizzly skies" and do like I do. Pretend you just had knee surgery and require an upgrade, and mad-dog the passengers all the way to Paris, ready for anything. Get one of those 100-pound camel jockeys and fill it with 50 ounces of vodka and 50 ounces of Red Bull. When you get to customs at Charles de Gaulle, you are good to go. They will sense something about you that is different from your typical yacht club polo lounge platinum silicone bleached land pimp devochka in search of the *je ne sais quoi* continental experience. Flash them a tasty dollar wad in raw cash like a Richmond crack dealer, and they will let you slide.

If they ask your business, tell them in a nasty Buford T. Pusser drawl: "I'm here to see a Texas Tornado demolish France."

CHAPTER 29

Training Tips with Bobke

Auto-immune necrotizing Teflon-brained electricians of the mind don't know squat about training. Training tips designed by some lab-coated yuppie who has formulated his theories by gazing across an ocean of neon-Lycra-clad chicken shit to face road rage spin-class devotees are bunk. So let a scar-tissued, hard-as-coffin-nails, crosswind-craving metal storm lead you onto the path of righteousness and physical annihilation.

Tip 1: Crashing is better than eating right. Eating right makes you feel good about yourself. That is the last dang thing you want. You want to feel absolute shitbag about yourself. Your self-esteem should be lower than a snake's belly at the bottom of a Deep South penitentiary septic tank.

When you have the appropriate base level of self-esteem, you'll want to inflict the grinding horror of your mind upon all around you. Appeasing the torments of your mind by ripping people's legs off in a bike race so you can be seen kissing the podium dolls is the best path. Eating right is better suited to actresses who've guzzled so many lies getting movie roles that their digestive enzymes have been vaporized.

Now, crashing, on the other hand, gives you scar tissue, and scar tissue tells a story no idiotic tribal barbwire tattoos ever will. And as the stories of your scars are retold, you'll get hungry for sour mash and pork rinds. It is almost impossible to eat a macrobiotic salad while picking at your scabs and describing your ass-over-tits, auger-into-the-gravel-pile-moving-into-sprint-position in the last corner. Self-hate propels the bicycle faster than all the 30/30/40 ratio flim-flam, phin-phen scam artists combined. Let retired generals, Enron satanists, Juan Exxon Valdez, and Guantanamo Bay-detained Islamic Jihadists eat right. It is way better to crash hard and eat wrong.

Tip 2: Lactate-threshold training is stupid. It is designed to enable your body to process exertion with less pain. Forget about it. Lactic acid is good. During the 2001 Tour, Victor Hugo Peña had more lactic acid in his legs than all the cows in Wisconsin. He didn't give a rat's ass. You should have more acid in your legs than Ken Kesey, Pigpen, Tim Leary, Ravi Shankar, and Peggy Lipton combined. The acid from your legs will seep into your belly and creep up your spine into your brain where it turns into hatred for the horrible tweakers who wrought this debilitation upon you. As the desperately loathsome creature you now see yourself as, you will want only one thing—revenge! And a biker who wants revenge is a truly dangerous beast.

Tip 3: Don't watch Tour videos. Watch Jerry Springer. Let the pathological madness of trailer-park white-trash teen-pregnant buck-toothed tobacco-stained whiskey-soaked crack-addicted sobbing lunatics capture your imagination. Contained within the demented desperation of misdirected rage lies the epiphanous revelation we seek. Tour videos blathering pithy exhortations about Big Mig's/Lance's/LeMond's glorious prowess ain't got shit on Jerry Springer. You can't learn how to paint by looking at Van Gogh's potato eaters, but you can taste the poverty etched into lines on the faces of mangled-by-labor Dutch serfs who look a lot like Erik Dekker and Michael Boogerd. Tour champions are bloated with adulation, and most couldn't give a good goddamn about it. The ones I've known would rather have a beer, some chips and salsa, and watch some swamp buggy monster truck demolition.

Tip 4: Bucolic group rides in the countryside near Boulder and San Diego make you weak. Detroit, Michigan; Gary, Indiana; or rural Texas are much better places to train. One solo ride dodging bullets from crips and cinderblocks pitched out of pickups by rednecks will do more for your training than all the yuppy scum wank fests parading through the Rockies and the PCH combined. Beer bottles full of shot peen whizzing past your ears sound much better than some trustafarian, vegan, scandium-clad, anemic, lifestylin' zombie of fitness spewing forth about the Q factor of Campy's latest all-carbon Record 10 cranks. You wanna get your heart rate above 200? Try out-sprinting a flat black 1963 Impala with Dayton wheels, hydros all around, slammed, louvered, frenched, chopped, four bodies in the trunk, full of AK-totin' gangsters on the streets of Chicago's Southside.

Tip 5: It is better to drink turpentine and eat creosote than eat PowerBars and drink Cytomax. You'll get sick. You'll get so sick you'll become sick. Sick is good. Good health is bad for a bike racer. If you are healthy, you aren't training hard enough. Healthy, wealthy, and wise is for ambassadors and Republican presidents, not bike racers. You *need* to be sick, poor, and stupid.

Tip 6: Volunteering at a convalescence hospital is better for your cycling than weight training. Weight training is for preening sissies whose brains have turned to mush as their muscles bulge. What a cyclist needs to be regularly exposed to is not a mirror-lined pneumonia-inducing Petri dish of human disease gym, but rather gut-wrenching tales of regret and the litany of wasted opportunity as only the abandoned elderly can tell.

Tip 7: Coaches are constantly telling athletes to train low and sleep high. Bobke says move to Belgium and race every day, or get high and don't train at all.

Tip 8: Do you wanna have the best race of your life? Do this every day for two weeks: (1) Wake up and eat one bowl of cereal. (2) Ride 100 miles. (3) Drink a shot of whiskey and an extra stout Guinness. (4) Nap until 8 p.m. (5) Eat one cheeseburger. (6) Sleep all night. (7) Take one day off and eat everything in the house. (8) Race the next day. You will be flying. Of course, you'll have to take a month off afterward.

CHAPTER 30

Il Becco Bartalese

Seguendo le orme di Coppi e Bartali

Bob Roll wrote this column in Italian to convey fully the unique ambiance of Italian cycling. The English translation follows.

Caffè Volta, Como, ore 9:07

Chiappa arriverà tra qualche minuto," spiega il mio amico Michele. Michele é barista e proprietario del Caffè Volta dove, ogni mattina, vado a bere un buon cappuccino. I miei compagni di squadra mi chiedono sempre, "Perchè bevi e mangi nello stesso posto ogni giorno?"

"Perchè," spiego io, "in questo modo posso far parte della vita italiana." Loro, peró, proprio non mi capiscono! Per un americano e incredibile che io possa portare Chiappucci, ad un piccolo caffé, il giorno dopo una gloriosa vittoria della Milano–San Remo.

Ogni mattina, passo al caffè Volta per trascorrere un po di tempo, mentre, bevo caffelatte, mangio panini e brioche, parlo della vita statunitense e del ciclismo professionistico al piu alto livello. Forse, ora, puoi capire perchè quando parlo di me ad un barista italiano, lui mi vede diverso, un pò strano rispetto agli altri atleti, forse fino al punto di credermi un po pazzo.

Chiappa non é mai in ritardo, ma oggi non si poteva nemmeno uscire dalla porta di casa per il casino fatto in onore Claudio sulla Milano–San

Remo. Finalmente, Claudio arriva al Caffè Volta in bici, anche lui, come sempre, vestito nello stesso modo degli altri corridori della squadra Carrera. Michele rimane subito paralizzato dallo stupore. Io gli presento la squadra ma lui non riesce nemmeno a parlare. Forse nessuno avrebbe portato un eroe del ciclismo mondiale, il più famoso personaggio della vita ciclistica italiana, ad un piccolo caffè, frequentato da un americano un pò pazzo. Michele riesce solo a fissarmi incredulo. Ora, per Michele, sono l'americano piu prestigioso del mondo ma, in realtà, io sono qui solo per vincere la corsa in bici e far parte della vita italiana di tutti i giorni.

Chiappa ed io, oggi, abbiamo seguito la strada che circonda il lago di Como. Quasi ogni macchina che passava gridava: "Forza Chiappucci," "Dai Chiappa," e così per centosettanta chilometri. Arrivati all'inforcatura del lago ci siamo arrampicati fino alla chiesa della Madonna del Ghisallo per far visita al cappellano che é vecchio decrepito ma, è stato felicissimo di vedere Claudio, alla cappella, subito dopo la Milano–San Remo. La gioia che ho visto nei suoi occhi é una cosa che non dimenticherò mai.

Non so se, per agli americani che corrono in bici qui, la vita italiana sia tanto interessante, ma siamo qui e io mi chiedo: Perchè non far parte della vita più bella del mondo? Perchè non assaporare la cucina italiana? Perchè non ricercare la gioia negli occhi dei vecchi e dei giovani? Questa gioia la potremmo trovare solo seguendo i passi di Coppi e del becco Bartalese.

☆　☆　☆

FOLLOWING IN COPPI'S AND BARTALI'S TRACKS

9:07 at the Caffè Volta

Chiappa will arrive any minute now," explained my friend Michele. Michele is both waiter and owner of the Caffè Volta where my morning routine begins with a cappuccino. This routine never ceases to shock my teammates. "Why eat and drink in the same café every day?" they never fail to ask.

"It is so that I can begin my day with a typical Italian routine," I explain. This philosophy always blows past them. The idea that an American would bring Chiappucci to a small Italian café—no less than one day after an astounding victory in Milan–San Remo—was nearly beyond belief.

I begin every day at a café, passing the time by drinking lattés, eating paninis and brioche, discussing life in America and the highest levels of competitive cycling. You may have already guessed that when I talk with Italian waiters, they see me a bit different from typical athletes—a bit strange, possibly even crazy.

Chiappa is notorious for punctuality, but today he could not even get out of the door because of the mob of fans lined up along the way between Milan and San Remo. He finally arrived on his bike, dressed, as always, like all the other members of the Carrera team. Michele was paralyzed in shock; he could not so much as introduce himself to the team. It was beyond reasoning for a cycling hero, one of the greatest Italian icons, to show up with his team at a small café to visit a crazy American. Michele can only stare at me in incredulity. After this morning, my status will be forever elevated in his eyes. For Michele, I am now the most prestigious American in the world, but really, I am simply here to win bike races and to take part in the Italian daily life.

Today, Chiappa and I ride down the road around Lake Como. Nearly every passing car had some excited passenger who leaned out the window to yell support. For 170 kilometers all we could hear was, "Break a leg, Chiappucci," and, "Dust 'em, Chiappa." At the crotch of the Y-shaped lake, we climbed to the church of the Madonna del Ghisallo to visit the abbot. Seeing the excitement in the eyes of the ancient abbot while talking with Claudio is something I will never forget.

Bobke II

I am unsure whether the Italian life interests your average American cyclist, but I constantly ask myself, Why not become a part of the world's most beautiful culture? Why not taste the Italian specialties? Why live a day without seeing the excitement with which those in their prime can infect the elderly? That joy can only be found following in the footsteps of Coppi and Bartali.

Most cyclists know Bob Roll is a man of many pursuits: former Tour de France racer and mountain bike competitor; training partner of Lance Armstrong during his comeback from cancer; columnist in *VeloNews*; television commentator, interviewer, and writer for the Outdoor Life Network; and a sometime coach, TV-commercial star, bit part movie actor, storyteller, and inspirational speaker. In fact, a Google search on the Web revealed no less than 1,200,000 references to the infamous cycling scribe. But—Bob would like this—only a dozen of the items were about him. Most of the other 1,199,988 were about "BOB Dylan, rock and ROLL" or similar "Bob" and "Roll" combinations.

Born in 1960, in Oakland, California, where he had a, shall we say, unusual childhood, he somehow gravitated to racing bikes and was living in a tent in Switzerland when he was picked up by the 7-Eleven cycling team in 1985 to ride the Giro d'Italia (he finished a remarkable 78th). He later lived and raced in Belgium, where he adopted his Flemish moniker, Bobke (pronounced "boob-ka"), and enjoyed a better-than-mediocre racing career.

His writing was "discovered" before the start of a Belgian classic race by a *VeloNews* editor, who spotted a poem Roll had written on the sidewalls of his racing tires. There followed the zany Roll Diaries—a sort of cycling Dead Sea Scrolls—that first focused on his adventures in the European peloton, and later on the off-road circuit after he swapped skinny tires for fat and moved first to Santa Fe, New Mexico, and then Durango, Colorado.